D0260988

Special Corporations and the Bureaucracy:
Why Japan Can't Reform

# Special Corporations and the Bureaucracy

## Why Japan Can't Reform

Susan Carpenter

First published 2003 by
PALGRAVE MACMILLAN
Houndmills, Basingstoke, Hampshire RG21 6XS and
175 Fifth Avenue, New York, N.Y. 10010
Companies and representatives throughout the world

PALGRAVE MACMILLAN is the global academic imprint of the Palgrave Macmillan division of St. Martin's Press, LLC and of Palgrave Macmillan Ltd. Macmillan® is a registered trademark in the United States, United Kingdom and other countries. Palgrave is a registered trademark in the European Union and other countries.

ISBN 1–4039–1655–1

This book is printed on paper suitable for recycling and made from fully managed and sustained forest sources.

A catalogue record for this book is available from the British Library.

Library of Congress Cataloging-in-Publication Data
Carpenter, Susan, 1943–
    Special corporations and the bureaucracy : why Japan can't
reform / Susan Carpenter.
        p.   cm.
    Includes bibliographical references and index.
    ISBN 1–4039–1655–1
    1. Government business enterprises—Japan.   2. Corporations,
Government—Japan.   3. Industrial policy—Japan.   4. Bureaucracy—
Japan.   I. Title.
    HD4313.C35 2003
    338.0952—dc21                                              2003040530

10   9   8   7   6   5   4   3   2   1
12   11   10   09   08   07   06   05   04   03

Printed and bound in Great Britain by
Antony Rowe Ltd, Chippenham and Eastbourne

# Contents

# List of Tables

# Acknowledgements

I would like to express my deep appreciation to Professor John Dawson, Professor John Henley, Mika Ito, Professor Sadahiko Kano, Professor Kazuo Usui and Dr Fabian Zuleeg for their support.

I also wish to thank Professor Paul Thompson for encouraging me to write the book.

SUSAN CARPENTER

# 1
# Introduction

This book reveals how the Japanese ministries can exploit special corporations in order to intensify their administrative power over industries and local governments, and to perpetuate the interests of elite civil servants by facilitating the migration to post-retirement positions in the private sector. The book explains why the existence of these organizations frustrates Prime Minister Junichiro Koizumi's efforts to initiate structural reforms.

Special corporations (*tokushu hojin*) are types of large public corporations supported primarily by public funding from the Postal Accounts Agency, the state-run banking system, and the Fiscal Investment Loan Programme (FILP), which is often referred to as Japan's 'Secondary Budget'.

Japan's national government ministries established special corporations after the Second World War to aid in the reconstruction of infrastructure destroyed during the war and to resuscitate industry. The corporations are linked to the industrial sectors under the administrative jurisdiction of each ministry. For example, the Ministry of Construction (renamed in 2001 the Ministry of Land Infrastructure and Transport) established the Japan Highway Corporation in 1956 to rebuild highway networks. The corporation awards contracts to construction companies and funds these projects through FILP.

The Ministry of Finance established the Japan Development Bank (JDB) in 1953 to aid in Japan's economic recovery. The Ministry of International Trade and Industry (MITI) (renamed in 2001 the Ministry of Economy, Trade and Industry) founded the Japan Finance Corporation in 1955 to give long-term, low-interest loans to small

1

businesses. Again, the loans are funded by FILP. Another special corporation, the Japan National Oil Corporation, was established by MITI in 1967 to aid Japanese oil companies in the search for petroleum and natural gas supplies. Special corporations that have international recognition are giant organizations such as the Japan Broadcasting Company (NHK) and Japan Telephone and Telegraph (NTT).

Officially, the ministries do not manage their corporations, but in general the Japanese are aware that the ministries manage corporations *de facto* through the officials, who are sent to fill upper management positions.

By 1972, Japan had achieved an astounding annual growth rate of 10 per cent gross domestic product (GDP). Realistically, by that time, many of the special corporations were no longer necessary to support economic growth and rebuild the infrastructure, and, ideally, they should have been dismantled. However, the ministries had come to rely on their corporations, because not only did they provide post-retirement positions for officials, but they also served to extend ministerial powers and to increase administrative jurisdiction (namely, 'territory').

## The maze of public corporations

There are, at the time of writing, seventy-seven special corporations. There is a much larger category of public corporations (*koeki hojin*) that are classified as associations (*shadan*) and foundations (*zaidan*), the number of these being estimated as greater than 26,000. Approximately 6,879 corporations are managed by central government agencies and the rest are managed at the local government level. The number of associations and foundations differ from ministry to ministry. The Ministry of Education (renamed in 2001 as the Ministry of Culture, Sports, Science and Technology in 2001) has the largest number (over 1,800) with the Ministry of Finance and the Ministry of Economy, Trade and Industry coming a joint second with around 900 each.

Chartered corporations (*ninka hojin*) are yet another type of public corporation managed at the national level, such as the Central Bank of Japan, the Japan Red Cross, the Centre for Marine Technology, the Mutual Aid Society of Local Government Employees, and the Chamber of Commerce and Industry. Chartered corporations are similar to special corporations in terms of size, but they are not subject to evaluation by the Cabinet or the National Diet. Before 1970, Japanese connected to private industry established chartered corporations with the consent from the ministries. However, from 1968 onwards, the ministries began to establish such corporations at their discretion (namely, by ministerial ordinance), and by 1978 there were ninety-nine chartered corporations but the numbers slowly decreased through dissolution, privatization or consolidation to eighty-seven at the time of writing. In total, there are 163 special corporations and chartered corporations receiving ¥5 trillion in tax revenue in 2001.

Although the number of special corporations may seem insignificant in relation to the overall number of public corporations, many public corporations are subsidiaries of special corporations. Indeed, special corporations tend to breed more public corporations, providing post-retirement positions for elite civil servants and consuming public funds. In his book *The Parasites That Are Gobbling Up Japan: Dismantle All Special Corporations and Public Corporations* (*Nihon wo Kuitsuku Kiseichu Tokushu Hojin Koeki Hojin wo Zenhai Seiyo!*) (2001) Koki Iishi claims that special corporations have 2,000 subsidiaries and that these organizations employ about 10,000 people.

The Japanese civil service system permits retiring officials to take higher management positions in industry while at the same time receiving benefits from their former ministries. Known as *amakudari*, or 'descent from heaven', the movement of former bureaucrats to the private sector can forge a link between retired officials and officials in the ministries, and thus promote close co-operation between industry and the bureaucracy. To Western observers, this tight relationship between the ministries and industry has appeared to be a major strength of the Japanese political economic system. However, in reality, these networks act to rigidify the system, thus inhibiting the adaptation to the demands of the constantly changing environment of the global economy.

The National Public Service Law stipulates that retiring civil servants must wait for two years before taking positions in corporations in the sectors their ministries manage. Nevertheless, they may move directly to higher management positions in special corporations and other types of public corporation, receiving salaries simultaneously from their ministries and from the public corporations. Most officials

*Public corporation ⟶ private companies.*

will wait out the two-year period of grace in public corporations and then slip into higher management positions in private companies. It is generally understood that civil servants like to establish public corporations in order to carve out positions for themselves and their colleagues.

The Japanese, since the 1890s, have traditionally depended on their elite civil servants to plan and implement economic and industrial policies, and the bureaucracy is the most influential body in Japan's governing system. Until the asset-inflated economic bubble burst in 1990 it was believed that elite civil servants had created an economy that appeared to be impervious to failure. The Japanese generally accepted *amakudari* because it was one of the incentives that attracted talent into the ministries, where the retirement age can be ten years earlier than in the private sector, and where salaries and benefits were lower than those earned by corporate executives. However, from 1992 onwards the stagnation of Japan's economic growth, coupled with the revelation of collusion between the Ministry of Construction and the construction industry, and between the Ministry of Finance and the banking industry, triggered a political movement by opposition parties to regulate or abolish the *amakudari* system. In addition, there were growing demands that all special corporations be dismantled, or at least the number drastically reduced, not only because some have massive debts and are a drain on public funds but also, equally, they are the vehicles that civil servants use to migrate smoothly into positions in private companies.

## The murky side of special corporations

*The character of special corporations*

The conditions for the establishment of special corporations are unclear. Most Japanese know very little about special corporations except that they are prolific employers and big spenders. Even the government has difficulty in defining the exact characteristics of special corporations other than that they assist the government in promoting national interests.

Although the government has not defined special corporations clearly, they can be viewed as being corporations based on a national law which has been approved by the National Diet. Special corporations were established according to special establishing procedures through a special law, the Law Establishment Act, Article 4-11 subject to the Ministry of General Affairs (renamed in 2001 the Ministry of Public Management, Home Affairs, Posts and Telecommunications). The law is neither civil nor corporate. For example, the Japan Highway Corporation was founded according to the 'Japan Highway Corporation Law', the Japan Development Bank was established through the 'Japan Development Bank Law', and the Japan National Oil Corporation was established according to the 'Japan National Oil Corporation Law'.

## Structural reform and the streamlining of public corporations

During the 1990s in an attempt to ignite Japan's stagnant economy, its government released numerous fiscal stimulus packages that have, in fact, done little more than drain public funds. Prime Minister Koizumi's platform focuses on extensive reform of the state sector in an effort to reduce public debt, which was 130 per cent of GDP in 2001 and climbed to 140 per cent of GDP in 2002. The reforms include the downsizing of FILP, the privatization of the Postal Accounts Agency, and cutting government funding to special corporations by a third. The Ministry of Public Management, Home Affairs, Posts and Telecommunications reported in 2002 that the streamlining of public corporations had begun in 1995 and that by 1999 numbers had decreased by fourteen. In 1997, eighty-four special corporations received ¥34 trillion 438 billion from Postal Savings. In 1999 they received ¥256 billion in subsidies from the National Treasury, and in 2000 the amount rose to ¥258 billion.

Koizumi aims to dissolve, privatize or convert into independent administrative institutions the 163 special corporations and chartered corporations. The fact that only fourteen special corporations have been dismantled is indicative of the stiff opposition Koizumi is facing from the ministries, in charge of administrating the reforms, and from members of his own party, the Liberal Democrats, who have dominated Japanese politics since 1955 and who have supported ministerial policies consistently. In fact, civil servants opt to leave the ministries to run for political office, often on the Liberal Democratic ticket, which is also considered to be amakudari. With this kind of support mechanism in place it is highly unlikely that the ministries will feel any pressure to relinquish their organizations.

### Why Western academics have not conducted extensive research on public corporations ⓵ —

Japan's depressed economy has convinced Japanese citizens that they can no longer sustain public corporations. Since the mid-1990s as the Japanese economic crisis has continued unabated, a plethora of books and articles by Japanese commentators, media and politicians from the opposition parties have been published, calling for the dissolution of public corporations because they advance the vested interests of the ministries and an obsolete civil service system.

Japanese authors write from the perspective that the duties the government assigned to public corporations in the 1950s and 1960s, such as the allocation of funds for construction contracts and the issue of low-interest mortgages should be done directly by the government or private institutions. These commentators write that public corporations have come to serve as the main vehicles facilitating the smooth entry of civil servants into the private sector, thus perpetuating the link between business and government. Yet Western commentators have written little about this key factor that serves to bind the political and economic system together, thus inhibiting reforms.

The paucity of literature is a result of several factors. Until the Law Concerning Access to Information Held by Administrative Organs was enacted in 1999 there was a minimum of information regarding how public corporations operated in terms of annual expenditure, how the corporations used their budgets, and the sources of the funds. In other words, operations were concealed from public scrutiny. The information available to the public about public corporations relatively is still scanty because the organizations are not required to reveal all if they receive funds other than tax revenue. Also, accounting systems used by public corporations differ from those of private corporations.

Second, until only recently, Western commentators believed that Japan's economy was strong and enduring. They believed generally that the bureaucracy was responsible for forging policies that spurred Japan's post-war industrial rebirth and rapid economic growth, challenging American industries in global markets. Economists and scholars alike looked in wonder at what had come to be known as Japan's 'economic miracle'. As Japan's economy grew, so did the number of academics and journalists who wrote commentaries and books that focused on defining the elements comprising the Japan 'model', a recipe for success.

Unfortunately, most commentators did not temper their enthusiasm for Japan's 'model' with a word of caution that Japan's seemingly unstoppable economic growth was related directly to a system consisting of traditional institutions specific to Japan's political economy, and institutions that had been established precisely to underpin Japan's industrial resuscitation. In the 1970s and 1980s, in order to take advantage of the growing interest in the Japanese model, and anticipating a substantial profit from a higher student population, universities established centres for the study of Japan and Japanese culture. Business schools added Japanese-related fields, students learnt the difficult Japanese language, travelled to Japan through Japanese-government-sponsored exchange programmes to see what they were allowed to see of the Japanese system. Japanese private corporations contributed large endowments to well-known universities where employees and ministry officials were sent to receive degrees in business administration and law, as well as to build formal and informal networks with academics and future CEOs. Educators' perceptions of Japan's economic and social conditions were influenced by the data released to them by government-financed corporations and their respective spokespersons. It is also tempting to conclude that close observation of ministerial objectives in the use of public corporations has been discouraged, since some special corporations and other public corporations fund selected foreign scholars' research in Japan and provide economic and social data as a means of promoting their legitimacy.

The main body of literature on Japan's political economy has simply defined elements in the governing system that were once considered to be the principal reasons for Japan's economic might. Emphasis was placed on the power of the bureaucracy and the domination of a single political party. *Amakudari* was defined as the migration of former bureaucrats to positions in the private sector where they forge an abiding relationship between government and business, hence the coining of the term 'Japan Incorporated'.

Since the mid-1990s, analysts have written prolifically about the reasons for the rupture of Japan's asset-inflated 'bubble' economy.[1] However, in 1988, many seemed oblivious to the looming rupture of the real estate and stock markets, preferring to focus on Japan's trade surpluses and seemingly dynamic economy. Even though Japan was the world's largest creditor, the economy was clearly overheated and the Japanese themselves were referring to their economy as a 'bicycle economy' (*jitensha keizai*) because they had to pedal continuously to keep it going at high speed. Competition among domestic firms to woo consumers with a constant flow of new products was evident in the market place. If one product did not meet with consumer acceptance within a brief period it was pulled from the shelves and replaced with another. Publishers launched magazines but would discontinue them after the first few issues if they did not sell immediately.

Banks were encouraged by the Ministry of Finance to lend money to manufacturers for investment in new equipment with the expectation that there would be an upsurge in demand. Borrowing from banks was an easy matter even though borrowers might have put up collateral that had already been used for that purpose. Big Japanese companies invested heavily overseas, opening factories throughout the United States and Europe, and small businesses followed suit. The strategy was logical because the government and businesses anticipated a rise in consumer demand for products ranging from processed foods to motor vehicles. Raw materials were also cheaper abroad than in Japan where natural resources, such as fossil fuel, are in short supply. Japanese speculators and large corporations bought up high-profile property at inflated prices.

Even in 1992, although Japan was in recession and clearly beset with grave economic problems, analysts of the Japanese economy remained very positive about its future recovery. Japan's economic woes were attributed to macroeconomic reasons emanating from inflated property and stock prices. The possibility that major structural problems in the Japanese governing system itself were contributing factors was generally not considered until fiscal stimulus packages not only failed to ignite the economy but also sent government debt rocketing.[2] There was little recognition that the network of bureaucrats throughout business and political communities acted to ossify the political economic system and was a major factor for Japan's inability to take the necessary measures to salvage its economy. Little heed was paid to how public corporations could operate as extensions of the ministries and as organizations that promoted the interests of elite officials.

Chalmers Johnson is the only Western commentator on Japan who has written about special corporations: *Japan's Public Policy Companies* was published in 1978. He also wrote briefly about public corporations (he used the term 'special status companies') in connection with *amakudari* in his fine book *JAPAN Who Governs?*(1995). He stated that public corporations extended ministerial powers but he admitted that non-Japanese scholars had conducted little research in this area.[3] Although other commentators have followed suit with articles that mention *amakudari* in public corporations, they generally explained how the migration process worked without analysing the effects of the migration.

While realizing that the Japan model is not as strong as they once believed, the majority of commentators are now writing about the need for reform in such areas as finance and education. However, they do not seem to appreciate that the very nature of the Japanese social political system frustrates reform, that two key mechanisms which glue this system together are public corporations and *amakudari*, and that before any lasting reform can take place most public corporations must be dismantled or privatized, and the civil service system must be revised so that *amakudari* can be abolished.

## Accessing information: the constraints on investigation

The efforts of academics and journalists to access comprehensive and reliable data about Japan's economy is complicated by the insularity of organizations and their reticence to open their doors to either Japanese or non-Japanese observers. The Japanese social political system is relatively opaque compared to Western industrialized nations, and gaining a solid understanding of a given environment can be difficult and time-consuming. This is particularly true of ministerial operations, because the ministries are very protective of their territory and control the flow of information tightly.

A further problem is that foreign observers are confronted by the language barrier. Several organizations have been formed by concerned Japanese citizens to keep a watch over the progress of reforms of special corporations and operate websites to inform the public, but these sites are in Japanese only. Government agencies control the release of most of the information regarding reforms, but only a small portion has been translated into English.

Both public and private corporations prefer to use special representatives, who are fluent in English, to communicate with researchers. Karel van Wolferen calls these representatives 'buffers,' and describes them as 'a peculiarly Japanese institution and readily recognizable in government offices as well as business corporations'.[4] Many of these representatives have been sent to universities abroad not only to study but also to interact with foreigners so that they can develop the skills to engage with foreigners on behalf of their organizations. Van Wolferen's other term for 'buffer' is 'propagandist,' but this is a rather unfortunate appellation because representatives believe it is their responsibility to protect their organizations' interests and fend off criticism. Japanese observers, who are not participants in the organizations they wish to observe may also be dealt with by these representatives.

Daily press coverage of government and private industry is relatively homogenous because the government can control the flow of information to journalists through press clubs. Also, newspapers and television will acquiesce to self-censorship because of their links with government and business.[5]

Japanese journalists and writers have difficulty in accessing up-to-date materials and most often rely on information released by government agencies some two to three years later. This is particularly frustrating for investigative writers because often the only sources available are government-generated data. They are also reticent about citing sources by name, referring to sources by job description and place of employment. Surprisingly, even popular weekly and monthly magazines such as *Bungeishunju* and *Sentaku* that have done excellent investigative reporting on the bureaucracy prefer to acknowledge authorship as 'staff writers' rather than including the names of their journalists.

All journalists covering government activities are assigned to press clubs, which are allowed to cover only certain bureaux. Bill Whittaker was the chief correspondent for CBS Television from 1989 to 1993. When he was interviewed by the author in 1994 regarding the difficulties of accessing information from Japanese government agencies he said that, compared to the United States, Japan was not as open and that the bureaucracy controlled information, revealing only what it chose. If he and his fellow journalists, both foreign and Japanese, wanted to cover a story about bureaux other than the ones to which they had been assigned they were confronted by barriers and would usually not pursue the story. Whittaker called the environment in the United States more 'porous'.[6] Judging from Whittaker's and other journalists' experiences, the most effective way to gather data is to develop an extensive network, but building this up can take years of effort.

Akio Mikuni and R. Taggart Murphy related in their book *Japan's Policy Trap*,[7] that scholars and analysts have difficulty in accessing reliable data concerning bureaucratic policies because there are no records of court cases, debates, or hearings as there are in the United Kingdom. Even politicians in high places have experienced difficulty in getting to the truth. They provided the example of Naoto Kan, the leader of the Democratic Party of Japan, the largest opposition party in Japan, when he served as minister of Health and Welfare in Prime Minister Ryutaru Hashimoto's coalition government. Kan was investigating the Ministry of Health and Welfare's complicity in the distribution of blood tainted with HIV that had been given untreated to haemophiliacs in the mid-1980s. Although Kan finally persuaded ministry officials to divulge information, he was asked not to make it public. Nevertheless, to the consternation of the ministry, he revealed all.

## Outline of the book

Chapter 2 defines Special Corporations. To illustrate the difficulties that Prime Minister Koizumi faces implementing the streamlining of special corporations, accounts are given of special corporations that have been targeted for elimination but are still operating. The views of opposition parties and Japanese commentators regarding special corporations are discussed to point to a growing public dissatisfaction with ministerial conduct and the concerns that reforms will not take place unless all public corporations are dissolved. Included is a table (2.1) that lists the 77 special corporations with the numbers of board members and employees, the salaries of the chief executive (if available) and website addresses. A second table (2.2) is provided to show the profit–loss accounts of the corporations where such information has been made available to the public.

Chapter 3 explains the origins of bureaucratic power from a historical perspective and the development of its close relationship with big business before the Second World War.

Chapter 4 summarizes Japan's post-war governance system set up by the Supreme Command of the Allied Powers, to show how America's post-war policies continued to give Japan's bureaucracy extraordinary power to administrate the country's economy. The support that Japan's dominant political party receives from interest groups in the ministries' respective administrative jurisdiction is explained with reference to two special corporations. In addition, there is a section discussing the opinions of the Japanese themselves regarding their bureaucracy, and a profile of the elite bureaucrats who regulate Japan's economy.

Chapter 5 discusses the network of interpersonal relationships in Japan's socio-political system that act to create an organic dependence between the bureaucracy, business and politicians. The policy instrument 'administrative guidance' is explained, showing how the network of retired bureaucrats in private businesses and their former colleagues in the ministries exerts pressure on companies to comply with regulations. Examples are provided to illustrate how a governor of a rural prefecture used his interpersonal network with central government officials to procure subsidies from central government and how a medium-sized business owner benefited from his connections in government and big business to procure subsidies and to expand his company's operation overseas.

Chapter 6 explains the *amakudari* system in both business and politics, and how it functions to create a network of elite civil servants throughout Japan's political society, intensifying ministerial power but also ossifying the political economic system. It shows how public corporations assist elite officials to migrate to private corporations, and how both large and small firms use retired officials to forge pipelines to the central ministries, thus facilitating subsidies, contracts, and applications for patents and licences.

Chapter 7 is a study of the Japan External Trade Organization, one of the twelve Special Corporations managed by the Ministry of Economy and Industry (METI). The corporation, with seventy-nine overseas branches and thirty-six domestic offices, is an appropriate example of how ministries can use their corporations to snatch away territory from other ministries and re-orchestrate the functions in order to keep them in operation.

The Conclusion in Chapter 8 assesses Japan's economic situation at the time of writing and predicts the outcome of Koizumi's reform plans.

On 6 January 2001 some of Japan's ministries were consolidated. For example, the Ministry of Construction (MOC) and the Ministry of Transportation merged with the National Agency and the Hokkaido Development Agency to form the Ministry of Land, Infrastructure and Transport. Some of the ministries remained independent, but their names were revised. The Ministry of International Trade and Industry's (MITI) name was changed to become the Ministry of Economy, Trade and Industry (METI). In this book, if events occurred before 2001 the ministries that underwent name changes are referred to by the names they held at that time.

## The literature and reference material

Since there is little information regarding special corporations outside of Japan, books by Japanese commentators, Japanese newspapers and magazines are the primary sources of information related here. Government-generated material collected from the websites of various agencies is also cited, along with the website address of each agency. Some of the agencies have translated their websites into English. Readers should be cautioned that the information from government sources, especially statistics and in some cases accounting data, may be incomplete and, therefore, unreliable. In April 2000, the late Prime Minister Keizo Obuchi called for a total overhaul of the methods by which statistics are collected in Japan after discovering that the figures for Japan's annual GDP were incorrect as a result of the ways that data were collected. The Economic Planning Agency (EPA), the main collection agency of macroeconomic data, had to make major revisions to the statistics it released on Japan's GDP. There were also discrepancies in the monthly and quarterly figures. Additionally, figures were released that portrayed production as having increased to show that demand was strong, while the EPA's statistics revealed that demand had declined.

# 2
# Special Corporations: On and On They Go

Special corporations receive funds through investments from postal account savings[1] and funds, and loans from the Financial Investment Loan Program (FILP), often referred to as Japan's 'secondary budget'. FILP was established in 1953 and can be described as a huge financial organ operated by the public sector. Postal savings is its largest part with another entity being the public pension fund.[2] Tax revenue from both national and local governments also is a source of funding and supplementing of budgets.[3] Although four special corporations operate independently of tax revenue, forty-five corporations depend entirely on it. Seven corporations use over 90 per cent tax revenue, three use more than 80 per cent, one receives 70 per cent of its funding from this source, two operate on 60 per cent tax revenue, and one receives less than 50 per cent.[4] Since the funding for some of the corporations does not come entirely from tax revenue (for example, private investment) they are not required to make public the sources of other capital investment.

Kan Kato was the Director of Chiba Commercial College when *Nikkei Business*, Japan's largest business weekly, interviewed him for its February 1997 cover story on special corporations. He emphasized that public funding of special corporations was a serious problem because the ministries have the power to use the money at their discretion without seeking the consent from the Diet. Indeed, politicians support this behaviour because they solicit contracts from special corporations involved in public works for their constituents.[5] Generally since 1955 an obliging National Diet has supported the

14

ministries' policies continuously and bureaucrats have operated relatively independently from legal sanctions.

## Public disclosure

The Law Concerning Access to Information Held by Administrative Organs[6] was enacted in 1999. Article 42 Information Disclosure by Independent Administrative Institutions and Public Corporations stipulates: 'in accordance with their character and type of business, the government shall take necessary measures such as legislative measures relating to the disclosure and provision of information held by independent administrative institutions and public corporations'. Prior to 1999 the ministries were not obliged to make public the budgets or operational expenses of their organizations.

At the time of his interview, Kato stated that there was no public disclosure by special corporations for accounts (for example, profit–loss balance sheet) and that the accounting system used was difficult to fathom because it differed from the system used by private corporations, and he recommended that special corporations be privatized. He complained that the subsidiaries of special corporations referred to as 'children and grandchildren companies' (*kogaisha* and *magogaisha*) also furnish post-retirement positions for former bureaucrats, but disclosure of this information was not readily available to the public.[7] The subsidiaries are included as public corporations. As an example of special corporation subsidiaries, the Electric Power Development Co. Ltd (EPDC), a METI special corporation has twelve. Among them are: EPDC Environmental Engineering Service Co. Ltd; EPDC Coal Tech and Marine Co. Ltd; Kaihatsu Co.; Kaihatsu Computing Services; Kaihatsudenki Co.; KEC Corporation; KDC Engineering Co.; and EPDC Overseas Coal Co. The EPDC also has a holding company and an industrial company.

Since Kato's interview, special corporations have opened their books to public scrutiny, or at least have revealed more than what was available before 1999. However, many other public corporations, including the subsidiaries of special corporations, have not opened their books.

Despite the new law, the government is still in the process of deciding how all types of public corporations will declare information regarding administrative activities. It claims that there is 'ongoing

effort' to disclose accounting and operations, and that there will
be an 'access room' where the public will be able to obtain data.
Nevertheless it is difficult to access up-to-date data. Although special
corporations have websites, the information provided on expenditures and sources of funding is sketchy and often not current. For
example, the Japan National Oil Corporation (JNOC), discussed later
in this chapter, has made public its balance sheet for March 2000.

## Public corporations: why so many?

As stated in Chapter 1, the official count of public corporations is a
little over 26,000 – an astounding number – and of these 6,879 are
managed at the national level and the remainder managed by local
government agencies. The numbers of corporations have gradually
increased since the end of the Second World War. For example, the
Ministry of Construction established ten corporations in 1950 and
by 1955 there were twenty-six. During Japan's period of rapid
growth, ten further public corporations were established annually. By
1960, the number had increased to fifty-two, by 1965 there were 102
and by 1970, the Ministry of Construction had established 144.
Another forty were added to the list by 1975, by 1980 the total was
240 and by 1990 the number had grown to 326. Among 322 of these
corporations, 34 per cent employed fewer than five people, 54 per cent
employed fewer than ten people, and only 9 per cent had more than
one hundred staff.[8]

Nevertheless, there is one corporation employing over 700
employees and it is one of the MOC's largest. Japan is often referred
to as the 'construction country' because of its unceasing construction of infrastructure and public works since the early 1960s
when Japan was preparing for the Tokyo Olympics. The Ministry
of Construction formed this public corporation – the Association
for the Establishment of Highways – in 1965 to make roads safer by
building rest areas, areas where bikes could be repaired and petrol
stations. The corporation now engages in building loading and service areas on highways. Its expenditures in 1998 were approximately
¥69 billion.[9]

The other ministries established public corporations at the same
rate or even faster than the Ministry of Construction, and it was a
simple procedure because all that was necessary to establish a new

one was the writing of an 'establish law' in the name of the corporation and a request to an obliging Diet to sanction it.

## Dissolution but in name only

In 1999 the government released a schedule[10] detailing the progress for streamlining special corporations according to its definition of these. The schedule identified the corporations that had been dismantled prior to 1996, when their number stood at ninety-two. As of October 1999 there were eighty-four corporations:

   (i)   twelve *kodan* – corporations that engage in public works projects
   (ii)  sixteen *jigyodan* – corporations that can be involved in just about anything except construction
   (iii) nine *koko* – corporations in public finance
   (iv)  two *ginko* – banks
   (v)   one *kinko* – a corporation where loans are made from capital supplied from both the public and private sectors
   (vi)  one *eidan* – a type of corporation that was commonly established during the Second World War, receiving both private and public funding. After the war *eidan* became known as *kodan*
   (vii) twelve *tokushu kaisha* – corporations that are funded with both public and private funds such as Japan Airlines
   (viii) the largest group of special corporations called 'others' (*sono hoka*) numbering twenty-five, their nomenclature illustrating the ambiguous nature of special corporations.

By April 2002 seven more corporations were privatized or dismantled, bringing the count down to seventy-seven.[11] One of the privatized special corporations was the Long-Term Credit Bank of Japan, established by MITI in the early 1950s. The bank was in financial trouble when Ripplewood, an American venture-capital company, purchased it in 1999. Two other banks that MITI had established in the 1950s as special corporations – the Japan Export–Import Bank and the Bank for Overseas Economic Co-operation – were consolidated in 1998.

It is interesting to note that most of the corporations that were dissolved had large outstanding loans and were merged with more solvent corporations. The names of the corporations they merged with have been changed, giving the impression that these corporations

春司上

were dissolved as well. Ostensibly the ministries are agreeing to part with some of their corporations, but they are, in fact, finding ways of maintaining them as illustrated by the Development Bank of Japan (DBJ). In October 1999, the Ministry of Finance's Japan Development Bank (JDB) merged with the bankrupt Hokkaido–Tohoku Development Finance Corporation, a regional *koko* and a special corporation managed by the ministry. The merger was celebrated with a new name, the Development Bank of Japan (DBJ). The bank's former name in Japanese translates as 'Japan Development Bank' (*Nihon Kaihatsu Ginko*) but although the new name in English appears to be almost identical, the Japanese translates as 'The Investment Strategy Bank of Japan' (*Nihon Seisaku Toshi Ginko*). Takeshi Komura, the bank's governor at the time of writing, in his 'Message from the Governor' avoids mentioning the dire problems that forced the JDP to take over the Hokkaido-based special corporation. It is conceivable that people in Japan will think that the bank is new and forget about the outstanding loans of the Hokkaido–Tohoku Development Finance Bank.[12]

## Koizumi's proposed reforms to cut public spending

In June 2001, Prime Minister Koizumi targeted special corporations and chartered corporations for review. Julie Norwell, assistant editor for The Oriental Economist, reported in her 2001 December article that the government granted ¥5 trillion (US $42 billion) annually in subsidies to the 163 corporations but due to incurred losses, the government will be forced to invest another ¥11.3 trillion in the companies.[13] This sum does not include loans from FILP or Postal Savings to these corporations. On 19 December 2001 the government announced extensive plans to merge, privatize or convert them into independent administrative institutions (discussed later in this chapter), whose work will be closely scrutinized. 浄箏

Seiichi Ota, formerly the director of general affairs for the Coordination and Planning Agency, and at the time of writing the director of the Liberal Democratic Party (LDP) office for the promotion of reforms, contended that one-third of the funds allotted to special corporations by the government was wasted. In an effort to cut such waste, Koizumi requested the ministries to review how special corporations in debt were spending funds. Koizumi would like to cut funding by 50 per cent, but even among his Cabinet members he is experiencing resistance. His State Minister Nobuteru Ishihara recommended that only a third of the designated corporations should be considered for reform and, as a consequence, Koizumi lowered his original figure to ¥1 trillion.[14]

Koizumi is also pushing for the privatization of the Postal Savings Agency because of ambiguous methods used for dispersing funds to both FILP, whose accounting is said to be opaque,[15] and to special corporations. He intends to downsize FILP by 17.7 per cent, or ¥26.79 trillion, and to privatize the Postal Service and Postal Life Insurance.

Koizumi's proposals are pragmatic, because both the national and local governments' coffers are running dry partly because of the continuous release of fiscal stimulus packages throughout the 1990s. Public debt was 130 per cent of GDP in 2001 and escalated further in 2002 to a whopping 140 per cent of GDP. In a gallant effort to plug the drain, Koizumi proposed cutting government funds to special corporations by a third and scrutinizing closely how loans are made to the corporations.

Special corporations that are big spenders are those involved in construction and finance, such as the Urban Development Corporation, Japan Highway Corporation and the Government Housing Loan Corporation, Japan's leading mortgage lender. The Ministry of Construction established these. A large portion of the fiscal stimulus packages went towards subsidizing the construction of infrastructure such as roads, bridges, dams and housing. In the year 2000, government reported that FILP loaned these corporations ¥2.1 trillion and ¥10.4 trillion, respectively. However, these funds proved inadequate, and the Ministry of Finance was forced to admit publicly that these corporations had gone over budget, that they, as well as the Road Building Agency, needed subsidies to cover 'hidden costs', and that ¥5,000 billion of tax revenue would be tapped. This admission was testimony to the public who had placed their trust in the Postal Account Agency that FILP spending was out of control. Ironically, the privatization of the Postal Savings Agency depends on finding alternative solutions to the refinancing of these enormous loans because tax revenue alone cannot possibly cover them.

### Deeper In debt but in denial

Ruichiro Hosokawa, a former managing editor of *Mainichi News*, one of Japan's five national dailies, is currently a political commentator.

In an article in the 16 November 2001 edition of the English-language newspaper, the *Japan Times* he wrote that Japan's economy would fail if reforms were not initiated. Emphasizing that Japan's public debt had reached ¥666 trillion, he reminded readers that, prior to 1975, the construction of infrastructure had been paid for with tax revenue generated by Japan's economic expansion. After that the government began to issue bonds to finance infrastructure work such as roads and bridges. In 1976, the Japanese were enjoying a stable economy and tolerated government borrowing. However, despite the fact that Japan's economy is now depressed, both central and local governments are continuing to borrow with a continuing nod of approval from the Japanese people. Hosokawa contended that the current budget tax revenue accounted for ¥50 trillion, but that deficit-covering bonds were financing amounts up to ¥30 trillion. He warned that if the government continued to support half its budget with deficit-covering bonds, Japan would become bankrupt.

Despite the grim predictions for Japan's economic future, Koizumi is fighting an uphill battle to push through the streamlining of more public corporations even though the ministries have agreed in principal to dissolve or consolidate seven of them. The Japan Highway Corporation (JH), established by the Ministry of Construction, is a huge *kodan* that is deeply in debt and one of the seven corporations planned for consolidation. The JH, which Koki Iishi labels 'the world's largest general contractor,[16] handles the construction contracts for major highways and toll roads throughout Japan. In theory, the JH repays loans from FILP with revenue collected from highway tolls, but these tolls are not sufficient to cover the repayment of loans.

Hosokawa urged the dissolution of the debt-ridden JH for the following reasons: (i) its president, vice-president and directors were former officials of the Ministry of Construction and lacked management skills; and (ii) public corporations should not be allowed to operate at a deficit. He also contended: 'The highway corporation's top executives should resign and refrain from accepting their retirement allowances. The same can be said of other public corporations.'

The JH has over sixty subsidiaries, with such names as New Japan Highway Patrol, Sapporo Engineer, Hokkaido Highway Service, Sendai Highway Service, Number One Highway Service, Western Japan Highway Service, Highway Service Research, Japan High Car,

Highway Toll System, Highway Kobe, Niigata Highway Service, Osaka Highway Engineer and Osaka Highway Service. These subsidiaries are spread throughout Japan. In 1998, Osaka Media Port's expenditures were the highest at ¥20 billion.

The JH is still in operation and is a good example of the problems Koizumi faces in his efforts to reduce public debt. Originally, Koizumi wanted to merge the JH with three other debt-ridden public corporations – the Hanshin Expressway Corporation, the Metropolitan Expressway Public Corporation and the Shikoku–Honshu Bridge Authority, which carries massive debts. He then wanted to privatize the single entity and have it repay the outstanding loans within thirty years. Koizumi also wanted to cut government investment in road construction. Evidently the government ploughs ¥300 billion annually into highway construction. If Koizumi had his way 40 per cent of future roadwork would be frozen and many lucrative contracts cancelled.

Koizumi's plans were admirable but the implementation of them was frustrated by LDP members in the Diet who were fearful that consolidation would mean a significant loss of business for their constituents, many of them small-business owners who traditionally have supported the LDP with substantial contributions. They demanded that the debts of the Shikoku–Honshu Bridge Authority be separated from the other corporations, and that those local governments where the bridges are located share the burden of repayment with central government.

Aware that, in order to progress with any reforms, Koizumi had to soften his stance on repayment of loans, he has extended the thirty-year grace period to fifty years. Also, political pressures have succeeded in thwarting his plans for consolidation. After consolidation the corporation will be dismantled into smaller entities, which will be privatized.

As the director of the Council of Labor Unions for the Liaison With Special Corporations, Kazuma Tsutsumi was in the perfect position to observe how the ministries use special corporations. In his book *The Monster Ministries and Amakudari: White Paper on Corruption (Kyodai Kanryo Amakudari Fuhai Hakusho)*, Tsutsumi stated that a JH subsidiary, the Japan Highway Improvement Corporation, contributed to an LDP association called the National Political Society. Tsutsumi quoted an announcement made in the 18 March 1997 issue of the *Asahi Shimbun*, one of Japan's major dailies, that the corporation gave a total of ¥15 million to the society in 1995 and 1996.[17]

Koizumi also wants to dissolve the Government Housing Loan Corporation. Established in 1950 by the Ministry of Construction to provide mortgages at low interest rates it in fact competes with private financial institutions that cannot afford to loan money at such low rates. If Koizumi's proposal is approved by the Diet, the corporation is supposed to be privatized by 2007. Its loan activities have been reduced gradually since 2002 (for example, funding from FILP is decreasing). So far no decision has been made concerning whether or not the corporation should be involved in loans after it is privatized because of the competition with private financial institution, but it most probably will be involved in securing home loans.[18]

## Holding on to a good thing

Koizumi would like to privatize the Japan National Oil Corporation because of outstanding loans totaling £7.8 billion, a debt that had not been divulged until the corporation was targeted for restructuring in 1998. The president, Kuni Komatsu, resigned after he announced the deficit.[19]

The Japan National Oil Corporation (JNOC) was established by MITI in 1967 to assist Japanese oil companies with exploration and drilling for oil. The corporation receives funds and loans from FILP. The JNOC has 142 affiliates and METI has proposed the sale or dissolution of seventy. According to the current plans the debt-ridden Japan Oil Development Co. will merge with Inpex Corporation and Sakhalin Oil and Gas Development Co.

The Japanese must import 99 per cent of their fossil fuel. METI oversees the energy-producing industries, among them oil. The ministry controls its import and refining through federations of oil importers such as the Kagoshima Federation for Oil Exploration, Federation of Oil Producers, Japan Petrochemicals and so on. These federations connect METI to the oil refiners, who distribute to retailers. The domestic companies co-operate with foreign oil companies to engage in exploration, production and refining of crude oil with the foreign firms usually holding the larger share of the investment.

One of the complaints lodged against the JNOC was that METI officials took temporary positions for two years and forged relationships with both foreign and domestic oil companies, which led to permanent post-retirement positions in these companies.[20] Traditionally, the president is an official of METI, but retired officials from MOF may fill other positions, such as vice-president or director of finance. Komatsu retired from METI in 1986. Before he became president of the JNOC he was an adviser in the now defunct Long-Term Bank of Japan, a Ministry of Finance special corporation. Currently there are two *amakudari*-generated positions for METI officials, two for officials from the Land Management Agency, and one for officials from the Small and Medium Enterprise Agency and the Institute for Accounting Research, respectively.[21]

METI claims that the privatization of the JNOC is scheduled for March 2005, however, the plans will not be finalized until they are reviewed by oil industry officials.

## Political opposition to special corporations

In 1992, the recession and the acknowledged need for action to ignite Japan's lagging economy triggered a struggle for power among factions in the Liberal Democratic Party, resulting in some members defecting to form two new parties, the New Japan Party (*Shin Nihon*), led by Morihiro Hosokawa and the Pioneer Party (*Sakigaki*), led by Ichiro Ozawa. In August 1993, Hosokawa, a former governor of Kita-Kyushu, was appointed to the office of prime minister, raising the hope among Japanese citizens that the government was going to deal with the recession and tackle political reforms. The government tried to jump start the economy by releasing several fiscal stimulus packages, much of the funds going to public works projects to give con tracts to businesses in the prefectures and to keep unemployment figures down. Unfortunately, after serving only eight months in office, Hosokawa resigned in April 1994 amidst rumours that he had accepted a loan from Sagawa Kyubin, a parcel delivery service whose previous loans to other politicians had caused a political scandal.

A struggle for power between the New Japan Party and the Pioneer Party ensued, revealing that there was serious disagreement among party members. Tsutomu Hata, a member of the New Japan Party who was the Minister of State, the Minister of Foreign Affairs and the vice-prime minister in Hosokawa's Cabinet, served as prime minister for four months. Tomichi Murayama, a Socialist, was appointed prime minister in July 1994. Forming a coalition Cabinet composed of members of the New Japan Party, the LDP and Socialist Party, he began to push for a review of bureaucratic powers and to attempt reforms of the political system itself in order to end the relationship between politicians, bureaucrats and businessmen, and thus bring Japan into the same league as other developed economic powers. This movement set off a power struggle between politicians and bureaucrats, who were intent on keeping control over the regulation of the economy.

Murayama's Administration suffered from a series of unfortunate incidents. The Kobe Earthquake on 17 January 1995 brought harsh criticism of government's handling of the aftermath. Political in-fighting, the continuing recession, and finally the attack of a young girl by American soldiers based in Okinawa encouraged voters to return to the LDP fold and this party began once again to dominate the Diet. Frustrated members of the New Japan Party and Pioneer Party gradually returned to the LDP or entered other long-established opposition parties. Nevertheless, the process for reform had begun.

Ryutaru Hashimoto, a conservative member of the LDP, succeeded as prime minister. When he served as the Minister of Commerce and Industry in Murayama's Cabinet and a member of the LDP he backed MITI's reluctance to participate in discussions regarding the downsizing of special corporations in 1995. During his three-year administration he proposed a plan to make government more efficient by regrouping the ministries and giving the prime minister's office more executive powers. On 6 January 2001, Hashimoto's plans were implemented with the consolidation of ministerial operations. However, at this time the extent of the restructuring seems to have applied mainly in the reshuffling of duties.

## Commentaries from opposition parties

Opposition parties have taken up the gauntlet calling for the reform of the *amakudari* system and special corporations. Comments from members of opposition parties reflect the dissatisfaction among the Japanese about their governing system, which they have come to regard as archaic and ineffective.

Yoshiki Yamashita, a member of the Japan Communist Party (JCP) who held a seat in the House of Representatives (Lower House) in the National Diet, releases a monthly column on his website that is linked to the JCP website. On 16 April 1998, Yamashita objected to elite ministry officials taking positions in special corporations, thus receiving substantial wages along with post-retirement benefits. He insisted that civil servants be prohibited from remaining in positions beyond a designated period of time. As an example of *amakudari* he pointed to one of METI's corporations, the Japan External Trade Organization (JETRO), where six out of the nine officials had moved from METI through the *amakudari* system.

In its 15 March 2001 issue of *Red Flag* the JCP, claiming that there were no regulations in effect that would limit the intimate relationships between retired civil servants and their former colleagues in the ministries, demanded that *amakudari* be abolished in both public and private corporations, and that a watchdog committee be set up to regulate it. The party also called for the initiation of a law requiring civil servants to wait at least five years before assuming positions in both public and private corporations and that when they moved to other corporations the salaries they received from their former corporations were terminated.

In October 2001, the strongest opposition party, the Democratic Party of Japan, together with the Socialist Party and the Free Party, called for a number of reforms that reiterated the demands of the JCP. The parties called not only for sweeping reforms of *amakudari* in both public and private corporations, but also restrictions on retired civil servants becoming members of corporate advisory boards.

Before his assassination by a right-wing sympathizer in Tokyo on 25 October 2002, Koki Iishi, a member of the Democratic Party of Japan, held a seat in the House of Representatives (Lower House) of the National Diet, serving as the chairman of the Special Committee on Disasters. He had been an exchange student at Moscow University from 1969–73. Iishi, who was a member of the New Japan Party, won a seat for the first time in July 1993 in the Lower House, serving as Parliamentary Vice-Minister of General Affairs. He entered the Democratic Party of Japan in 1996, winning a second term in the Lower House. He began a third term in June 2000.

Iishi, whose concerns centered on political and administrative misconduct, contended that special corporations and public corporations should be the focal point of structural reforms. In 1999, Iishi published a book about *amakudari* entitled *Bureaucrat Heaven: The Bankrupting of Japan* (*Kanryo Tenkoku Nihon Hassan*). He followed this in 2001 with a book on public corporations entitled *The Parasites That Are Gobbling Up Japan: Dismantle All Special Corporations and Public Corporations!* (*Nihon wo Kuitsuku Kisiechu Tokushu Hojin Koeki Hojinn wo Zenhaiseiyo!*)[22] Although his book may appear to be an effort on behalf of his party to weaken the bureaucracy and loosen the ministries' ties with the LDP, his report poses pertinent questions concerning the rapid escalation of public corporations that have been established through special corporations and government agencies, and the employment opportunities they offer to elite bureaucrats.[23] 和仏

When he assumed office, Koizumi's priority was to deal with non-performing loans and reforming the banking industry. Iishi had maintained that before structural reforms could progress, special corporations and public corporations that use public funds and tax revenue and serve *amakudari* should be dismantled.[24] He believed that there had been little movement towards reform of any kind. The reluctance of the ministries to reform special corporations and public corporations, thus preserving their territory, symbolized the rigidity of Japan's political economic system that inhibited reform.

Iishi claimed that public corporations employed 3.8 per cent of Japan's population or 4,900,000 people.[25] Iishi quoted the following statistics released in 2000 by the Management and Coordination Agency: (i) there were 6,879 public corporations managed by national government agencies, 35 per cent (or 2,428) of which employ 6,112 civil servants as managers, and (ii) 19,579 public corporations were managed by local government agencies, 29 per cent (or 5,631) of which employ 14,960 civil servants as managers.[26]

Iishi calculated that tax revenue allotted to special corporations in 1999 was ¥3,082,154 trillion compared with 1990 when public spending was ¥2,308,645 trillion.[27] Iishi agreed with Kato that special corporations bred subsidiaries, calling them 'family enterprises'.[28] He contended that there are 2,000 of these subsidiaries.[29] Iishi emphasized that, although the special corporations could be operating at a loss, their subsidiaries could be showing a profit, which could be divided among the parent company and the other subsidiaries. Iishi also pointed to public corporations established by local governments, which provided positions for local government officials. These organizations promote tourism, culture, education and agriculture. Iishi counted 6,615 former government officers in these organizations. He added that officers took temporary positions in these corporations, tallying 33,243 civil servants.[30]

Iishi tackled the problem of chartered corporations claiming that, like special corporations, they received investment from public funding and government subsidies and they bred subsidiaries. Also, chartered corporations received funds from associations that were managed jointly by local and national governments. Iishi indicated that the Ministry of Agriculture, Forestry and Fisheries had eight, the highest among the ministries. Some ministries managed between two to six corporations while others shared management.[31] Iishi contended that chartered corporations employed 100,000 people and provided post-retirement position for elite bureaucrats.

## Revelations by the Japanese media

Former Prime Minister Hosokawa's reform efforts opened the doors to close scrutiny by the news media of the ministerial use of public corporations. The numbers of books and articles critical of public corporations have increased as the economy has deteriorated.

The editorial staff of *Mainichi Shimbun*, one of Japan's five major dailies, entered the fray in 1994 with a book focusing on *amakudari* in both private and public corporations. *The Kasumigaseki[32] Syndrome (Kasumigaseki Shindorumu)*[33] is a surprisingly frank account of the deterioration of values among bureaucrats in terms of their objectives in establishing corporations and research institutes for the sole purposes of providing post-retirement positions for elite retirees.

The book's most significant contribution is the reporting on how *amakudari* and the temporary posting of elite officials in branch offices of special corporations in the prefectures (*shukko*) helped the ministries to monitor local government policies. Since the bureaucratic hierarchy places officers from the national ministries above local government officers, the positioning of ministry officials at the local government level automatically induces acquiescence by local government to ministerial guidance. The book was also critical of temporary postings because there was the ever-present possibility that the positions would become permanent.

The *Mainichi* staff detailed how ministries maintain control over their sectors by placing conservative elite retirees into management positions in both private and public corporations. In addition, they revealed how the ministries used special corporations to distribute funds to companies to cover contracts for public works, and how *amakudari* not only tied ministries to businesses but also facilitated connections between businesses and former bureaucrats, who move first to special corporations before moving on to the private sector.

The book includes a public survey, conducted in 1994, of 1,780 employees in seven special corporations that had been established by the Ministry of Construction. The employees were questioned about the *amakudari* of staff members, who comprised 80 per cent of the employees. The 7 per cent of the employees who answered that *amakudari* was still necessary were in the minority; 38 per cent felt that the system was a bad influence and should be abolished; 29 per cent felt that nothing much could be done about the situation because of the recession; 33 per cent claimed that the former bureaucrats were useless; and 50 per cent answered that the retired officials were helpful to some extent. Again, a minority of 3 per cent maintained that the former officers performed their duties well.[34]

By 1997, media coverage of special corporations had become heated. The February edition of *Nikkei Business* claimed that while special corporations were founded on the precept that the work executed would serve national interests the opposite was, in fact, true for the following reasons:

(i)   special corporations receive funding from sources that are difficult to trace.
(ii)  special corporations can set up subsidiaries (*kogaisha, magogaisha*) that show profits even though the parent corporations are in debt.
(iii) the ministries establish special corporations as their subsidiaries to provide temporary employment for staff and post-retirement positions for retired senior officials before they move to the private sector;
(iv)  special corporations spend funds to do work that is in the best interests of the corporations (for example, ministries).

## A watchdog organization has its say

The growing opposition to public corporations can be seen in the recent establishment of citizens' groups that maintain a vigil observing the progress of the reforms of special corporations. One of these organizations was established on 31 March 2000 and offers information on the Internet about special corporations. It is identified only by its website address 'Nomura'.³⁵ The March 2003 home page states that special corporations, chartered corporations, foundations and associations are the nucleus of a bureaucratic socialism created by bureaucrats. The reform of special corporations and public corporations is being closely scrutinized but real structural reform will not occur unless the bureaucratic society of this environment is destroyed.

*Nomura* reiterates the litany of complaints lodged by fellow opponents to special corporations. It points to *amakudari* as the keyword for understanding the problem of special corporations. The term 'syndicate' is used to define the lineage of 'children corporations', where elite bureaucrats move to positions after they leave special corporations. Questions are raised regarding the thoroughness of government audits, whether the corporations reveal all expenditure, profits and losses, and whether the Law Concerning the Access to Information of Administrating Organs is effective, since much of the funding is tied to tax revenue and to sources that are difficult to trace. *Nomura* looks at each special corporation in terms of effective use of funds. An appropriate example given is the Water Resources Development Public Corporation,³⁶ which *Nomura* takes to task for spending huge sums for the construction of dams that were not necessary.³⁷

The Water Resources Development Public Corporation's website home page welcomes visitors to 'J-Water Garden'. The corporation identifies itself as a special corporation established on 1 May 1961 and currently employing 1,900 workers. It discloses that government investment is a little over ¥2 billion. The corporation is the primary facilitator of river development projects in the country, its work focusing on the construction of dams.

*Nomura* goes into more detail, showing that the corporation was founded by the National Land Agency,³⁸ and that the MOC and the Ministry of Agriculture, Forestry and Fisheries are also involved. The payroll in 2001 was ¥29,080,000. *Nomura* contends that *amakudari* prevented private companies from participating in work projects with the Water Resources Development Public Corporation because other subsidiaries (where there are also *amakudari* positions) received a portion of the work. *Nomura* claims that out of the twelve positions in management, nine could be *amakudari*-generated. The website provided information for some of *amakudari* positions taken by ministry officials:

(i)   National Land Agency (3)
(ii)  Ministry of Agriculture, Forestry and Fisheries (2)
(iii) Ministry of Health and Welfare (1)
(iv)  Ministry of Finance (1)

*Nomura* claims that, although the corporation does not divulge the number of subsidiaries, there are such public corporations as the Association for Water Resources and the River Information Centre, where there are *amakudari* posts for officials. *Nomura* also voices concern that corporate expenditures rise annually while being supported by water charges and tax revenue.

*Nomura* tackles the special corporations that are involved in the promotion of horse racing, car racing, and bicycle racing[39] in Japan. These corporations are also managed and funded by local government. The corporations distribute a portion of their shares of the proceeds from ticket and event sales to their affiliate associations, which provide *amakudari* posts for bureaucrats who have moved from the establishing ministries. *Nomura* complains that the primary reason for transferring funds was to subsidize the affiliates so that they could maintain operations and thus providing post-retirement positions. *Nomura* also contends that the corporations failed to make public the amounts distributed.

## Independent administrative institutions: more image than substance? 実体

Koizumi's proposed reforms for special corporations have had the effect of weakening the stance of the opposition parties, who officially approved his proposed reforms of seven special corporations in November 2001. Koizumi has devised a scheme that will, in effect, convert thirty-eight special corporations and chartered corporations into independently administrative institutions (IAI), with the expectation that eventually financing from tax revenue will no longer be necessary. Similar to the 'law for the establishment of special corporations' the 'law for the establishment of independently administrative institutions' is neither a civil law nor a corporate law.

The Ministry of Public Management, Home Affairs and Tele-communications released an explanation in English that outlines the concept of the new IAI system:

> The IAI System lies on the basic concept of public welfare, trans-parency, and autonomy of activities as Article 3 of the Law of the General Rules provides that '(i) the IAIs must make efforts for the just and effective operation under the consideration that the fulfillment of their undertakings is indispensable from such public viewpoints as the stability of people's lives, society and the economy; (ii) the IAIs must make efforts to open to the public the status of their organizations and operations by such means as the announcement of the content of their activities as provided under this law; (iii) the autonomy of each law must be respected in accordance with the application of this Law and the laws estab-lishing the IAIs.[40]

Koizumi predicts that during the first decade of the twenty-first century the number of employees in the public service sector will decrease by 25,010 if the IAI system is implemented successfully.

There is no guarantee that Koizumi's plans will be successful, however, because the progress is going at a snail's pace. Although the House of Representatives (Lower House) had passed legislation to reform special corporations, the House of Councillors (Upper House) has, at the time of writing, yet to vote on the bill. At a press conference on 22 November 2002, Cabinet State Minister of Administrative and Regulatory Reforms Nobuteru Ishihara said he was hopeful that the bill would pass because the majority of mem-bers from the opposition parties in the House of Representatives had voted in favour. He stated that he would like Diet members to have a common understanding that the continuation of special corporations was problematic and that a detailed review was neces-sary. Pointing to JETRO as an example, Ishihara said that he was astonished to hear that the organization had a pamphlet adver-tising import promotion and that the Minister of Economy, Trade and Industry was equally shocked. Ishihara was implying that the importation of foreign goods was no longer a primary concern because of the recession and the contraction of the domestic market.[41]

JETRO is scheduled to become an IAI in October 2003. It was established in 1956 by MITI as a promoter of Japanese exports but in the 1980s, when Japan was experiencing a trade surplus with trading partners, the organization reversed its course to become a promoter of small businesses imports and international economic co-operation and, during the 1990s, a promoter of internal investment. In 2001, the corporation received ¥110 billion in government investment.[42]

So far the bureaucracy has been able to maintain its territory with the majority of special corporations in place. The government released the 'National Administrative Organization of Japan',[43] which refers to special corporations as 'public corporations,' stipulating that they are agencies of the national government. However, it qualifies this by stating that: 'their juridical person is different from the State. Therefore, the whole organization for the national administration covers an area larger than that of national administrative organizations of the proper sense of the term (Prime Minister's Office and 12 Ministries).'[44]

Despite Koizumi's good intentions, concrete reforms of special corporations will take years to implement, and tax revenue and public funding will continue to give support. The reform of the enormous special corporation Japan Telephone and Telegraph (NTT), which began in 1985, will take many years to reach completion. NTT was a monopoly when it began going through the process of privatization in 1985. Nevertheless, it was heavily regulated by the Ministry of Posts and Telecommunications. The NTT Law was revised in 1997 to permit it to engage in business oversees and to split up the corporation into NTT Holding Company and five major operating companies: NTT DoComo, NTT Data, NTT Communications (long distance and international service), NTT East (local service in eastern Japan) and NTT West (local service in western Japan). The NTT Group currently includes over 120 companies. The Ministry of Public Administration, Home Affairs, Posts and Telecommunications regulates three: the Holding Company, NTT East and NTT West. The two local companies have a monopoly on subscriber loops that connect users to the nearest telephone office. The holding company owns the largest number of shares in these companies.[45] The other companies are said to operate completely independently of regulation and compete freely with other domestic carriers. Nevertheless, the total privatization of NTT may take as long as twenty years more.

Former secretary general of the LDP and one of Japan's senior statesmen, Hiromu Nonaka stated at a news conference in Tokyo on 3 October 2001 that Koizumi's reforms did little more than indicate that certain organizations should change. He wondered how the problem of *amakudari* in public corporations could be addressed, since the chief cabinet secretaries of the ministries choose the officials to work in the corporations.[46] Nonaka contended that *amakudari* in special corporations was linked to the civil service system, suggesting that before the problem of *amakudari* could be solved, the civil service system must be restructured.[47]

Indeed, Nobuhiko Hiko, an economist and former reporter for the *Mainichi Shimbun*, claimed that senior officers in the ministries continue to make new public corporations and then 'dig up' posts in the corporations for fellow officers. As unemployment rises and the number of jobs offered to retired civil servants in the private sector decreases, ministries may become more possessive of special corporations and their subsidiaries.

*Table 2.1*   List of special corporations established by law, 1 December 2001

| Cabinet Office (3) | No. of board members | No. of employees | Established | Website URL | Yearly salary of top executive (estimated millions Yen) |
|---|---|---|---|---|---|
| 1 The Okinawa Development Finance Corporation | 5 | 220 | 15/05/1972 | http://www.okinawakouko.go.jp/ | 27.70 |
| 2 Association for the Restoration of the Japanese Kurile Islands | 2 | 19 | 01/10/1979 | http://www.hoppou.go.jp/ | 5.20 |

*Table 2.1 (Continued)*

| Cabinet Office (3) | No. of board members | No. of employees | Established | Website URL | Yearly salary of top executive (estimated millions Yen) |
|---|---|---|---|---|---|
| 3 Japan Consumer Information Centre | 5 | 117 | 01/10/1980 | http://www.kokusen.go.jp/ | 20.60 |
| **Ministry of Public Management, Home Affairs, Posts and Telecommunications (6)** | | | | | |
| 4 Postal Life Insurance Welfare Corporation | 4 | 2 292 | 27/04/1962 | http://www.kampo.kfj.go.jp/ | 25.63 |
| 5 Japan Finance Corporation for Municipal Enterprises (JFM) | 5 | 83 | 01/06/1957 | http://www.jfm.go.jp/ | 35.75 |
| 6 Nippon Telegraph and Telephone Corporation (NTT) | 11 | 3 165 | 01/04/1985 | http://www.ntt.co.jp | n.a. |
| 7 Nippon Telegraph and Telephone East Corporation | 15 | 48 250 | 01/07/1999 | http://www.ntt-east.co.jp | n.a. |
| 8 Nippon Telegraph and Telephone West Corporation | 15 | 50 450 | 01/07/1999 | http://www.ntt-west.co.jp | n.a. |

| 9 | Nippon Hoso Kyokai (Japan Broadcasting Corporation) (NHK) | 12 | 12 001 (March 2002) | 08/1926 | http://www.nhk.or.jp | 38.33 |
|---|---|---|---|---|---|---|
| | **Ministry of Foreign Affairs (2)** | | | | | |
| 10 | Japan International Co-operation Agency | 11 | 1 217 | 01/08/1971 | http://www.jica.go.jp | 27.83 |
| 11 | The Japan Foundation | 5 | 230 | 02/10/1972 | http://www.jpf.go.jp | 23.55 |
| | **Ministry of Finance (4)** | | | | | |
| 12 | National Finance Corporation | 8 | 4 779 | 01/06/1949 | httpi//www.kokukin.go.jp | 28.30 |
| 13 | Japan Bank for International Co-operation | 10 | 886 | 01/10/1999 | http://www.jbic.go.jp | 32.01 |
| 14 | Development Bank of Japan | 13 | 1 382 | 01/10/1999 | http://www dbj.go.jp | 21.00 |
| 15 | Japan Tobacco, Incorporated | 13 | 15 684 | 01/04/1985 | http://www.jti.co.jp | n.a. |
| | **Ministry of Education, Culture, Sports, Science and Technology (11)** | | | | | |
| 16 | National Space Development Agency of Japan | 8 | 1 090 | 01/10/1969 | http://www.nasda.go.jp | 24.75 |

*Table 2.1   (Continued)*

| | Cabinet Office (3) | No. of board members | No. of employees | Established | Website URL | Yearly salary of top executive (estimated millions Yen) |
|---|---|---|---|---|---|---|
| 17 | Japan Science and Technology Corporation | 7 | 466 | 01/10/1996 | http://www. jst.go.jp/ | n.a. |
| 18 | The Promotion and Mutual Aid Corporation for Private Schools in Japan | 7 | 1 261 | 01/01/1998 | http://www. shigaku. go.jp/ | 20.15 |
| 19 | Japan Scholarship Foundation | 6 | 471 | 20/04/1944 | http://www. ikuei.go.jp/ | 22.92 |
| 20 | Japan Atomic Energy Research Institute | 11 | 2 270 | 15/06/1956 | http://www. jaeri.go.jp/ | 30.30 |
| 21 | Institute of Physical and Chemical Research | 7 | 646 | 21/10/1958 | http://www. riken.go.jp/ | 25.80 |
| 22 | Japan Arts Council | 6 | 323 | 01/07/1966 | http://www. ntj.jac.go.jp/ | 21.00 |
| 23 | Japan Society for the Promotion of Science | 4 | 74 | 21/09/1967 | http://www. jsps.go.jp/ | 16.09 |
| 24 | Japan Nuclear Cycle Development Institute | 10 | 2 376 | 02/10/1967 | http://www. jnc.go.jp | 24.49 |
| 25 | The University of the Air | 6 | 315 | 01/07/1981 | http://www. u-air.ac.jp/hp/ | 19.90 |

| 26 | National Stadium and School Health Centre of Japan | 7 | 434 | 01/03/1986 | http://www. ntgk.go.jp/ | 21.40 |
|----|----|----|----|----|----|----|
| | **Ministry of Health, Labour and Welfare (8)** | | | | | |
| 27 | Labour Welfare Corporation | 6 | 13 875 | 01/07/1957 | http://www. rofuku. go.jp/ | 18.08 |
| 28 | Social Welfare and Medical Service Corporation | 6 | 267 | 01/01/1985 | http://www. wam.go.jp/ jigyoudan/ | 21.26 |
| 29 | Social Insurance Medical Fee Payment Fund | 4 | 6 399 | 01/09/1948 | http://www. shiharaikikin. go.jp/ | 9.00 |
| 30 | The Japan Institute of Labour | 5 | 138 | 15/09/1958 | http://www. jil.go.jp/ | 25.00 |
| 31 | Association for the Welfare of the Mentally and Physically Disabled | 4 | 310 | 11/01/1971 | http://www. nozomi. go.jp/ | 20.24 |
| 32 | Organization for Workers' Retirement Allowance Mutual Aid | 8 | 278 | 01/04/1998 | http://www. mmjp.or.jp/ | 30.09 |
| 33 | Employment and Human Resources Development Organization of Japan | 8 | 4 675 | 01/10/1999 | http://www. ehdo.go.jp | n.a. |
| 34 | Government Pension Investment Fund | 3 | 152 | 01/04/2001 | http://www. gpif.go.jp/ | n.a. |

*Table 2.1* (Continued)

| Cabinet Office (3) | No. of board members | No. of employees | Established | Website URL | Yearly salary of top executive (estimated millions Yen) |
|---|---|---|---|---|---|
| **Ministry of Agriculture, Forestry and Fisheries (7)** | | | | | |
| 35 Japan Green Resources Corporation (JGRC) | 7 | 825 | 16/07/1956 | http:// homepage1. nifty.com/ JGRC/ | 26.79 |
| 36 Agriculture and Livestock Industries Corporation (ALIC) | 11 | 166 | 01/10/1996 | http://alic. lin.go.jp/ | 10.39 |
| 37 Agriculture, Forestry and Fisheries Finance Corporation | 8 | 914 | 01/04/1953 | http://www. afc.go.jp/ | 28.30 |
| 38 Japan Racing Assoociation (JRA) | 13 | 1 851 | 16/09/1964 | http://www. jra.go.jp/ | n.a. |
| 39 Mutual Aid Association of Agriculture, Forestry and Fisheries Personnel | n.a. | n.a. | n.a. | http://www. norin-nenkin. or.jp/ | 9.00 |
| 40 The National Association of Racing | n.a. | n.a. | n.a. | http://www. keiba.go.jp/ | 26.38 |
| 41 Farmers' Pension Fund | n.a. | n.a. | n.a. | http://www. nounen.go.jp/ | 18.45 |

| | **Ministry of Economy, Trade and Industry** (12) | | | | | |
|---|---|---|---|---|---|---|
| 42 | Japan National Oil Corportion | 10 | 320 | 02/10/1967 | http://www.jnoc.go.jp/ | n.a. |
| 43 | Japan Regional Development Corporation (JRDC) | 12 | 665 | 01/08/1974 | http://www.region.go.jp/ | 10.50 |
| 44 | Metal Mining Agency of Japan | 6 | 183 | 20/05/1963 | http://www.mmaj.go.jp/ | 23.24 |
| 45 | Japan Small and Medium Enterprise Corporation | 11 | 912 | 01/07/1999 | http://www.jasmec.go.jp/ | n.a. |
| 46 | Japan Finance Corporation for Small Business | 8 | 1 668 | 20/08/1953 | http://www.jfs.go.jp/ | 28.10 |
| 47 | The Shoko Chukin Bank (The Central Cooperative Bank for Commerce and Industry) | 12 | 4 835 | 30/11/1936 | http://www.shokochukin.go.jp/ | 36.80 |
| 48 | Electric Power Development Co. | 21 | 3 323 | 16/09/1952 | http://www.epdc.co.jp/ | 29.00 |
| 49 | Japan Keirin Association | n.a. | n.a. | n.a. | http://www.keirin.go.jp/ | 29.00 |
| 50 | Japan External Trade Organization (JETRO) | 13 | 1 175 | n.a. | http://www.jetro.go.jp/ | 29.85 |
| 51 | Japan Auto Racing Association | n.a. | n.a. | n.a. | http://www.autorace.or.jp/ | 25.50 |

*Table 2.1 (Continued)*

| | Cabinet Office (3) | No. of board members | No. of employees | Established | Website URL | Yearly salary of top executive (estimated millions Yen) |
|---|---|---|---|---|---|---|
| 52 | Japan Nuclear Cycle Development Institute (same as No. 24) | 10 | 2 376 | 02/10/1967 | http://www. jnc.go.jp | 24.49 |
| 53 | New Energy and Industrial Technology Development Organization (NEDO) | n.a. | n.a. | n.a. | http://www. nedo.go.jp/ | 54.80 |
| | **Ministry of Land,Infra-structure and Transport (21)** | | | | | |
| 54 | Japan Highway Public Corporation (JH) | 9 | 8 632 | 16/04/1956 | http://www. japan-highway. go.jp/ | 38.61 |
| 55 | Metropolitan Expressway Public Corporation (MEX) | 8 | 1 368 | 17/06/1959 | http://www. mex.go.jp/ | 28.60 |
| 56 | Hanshin Expressway Public Corporation | 7 | 884 | 01/05/1962 | http://www. hepc.go.jp/ | 28.41 |
| 57 | Water Resources Development Public Corporation | 10 | 1 889 | 01/05/1962 | http://www. water.go.jp/ | 29.08 |

| 58 | Japan Railway Construction Public Corporation (JRCC) | 12 | 2 317 | 23/03/1964 | http://www.jrcc.go.jp/ | 35.44 |
|----|------|------|------|------|------|------|
| 59 | New Tokyo International Airport Authority | 8 | 890 | 30/07/1966 | http://www.narita-airport.or.jp/ | 38.83 |
| 60 | Honshu– Shikoku Bridge Authority | 7 | 452 | 01/07/1970 | http://www.hsba.go.jp/ | 38.83 |
| 61 | Japan Regional Development Corporation (JRDC) (Same as #43) | 12 | 665 | 01/08/1974 | http://www.region.go.jp/ | 10.50 |
| 62 | Urban Development Corporation | 13 | 4 712 | 01/10/1999 | http://www.udc.go.jp/ | n.a. |
| 63 | Corporation for Advanced Transport & Technology (CATT) | 7 | 140 | 01/10/1997 | http://www.catt.go.jp/ | 33.75 |
| 64 | The Government Housing Loan Corporation | 9 | 1 134 | 05/06/1950 | http://www.jyukou.go.jp/ | 27.80 |
| 65 | Teito Rapid Transport Authority | 13 | 9 880 | 04/07/1941 | http://www.tokyometro.go.jp/ | n.a. |
| 66 | Kansai International Airport Company Ltd | 10 | 523 | 01/10/1984 | http://www.kiac.co.jp/ | n.a. |
| 67 | Hokkaido Railway Company | 13 | 9 203 | 01/04/1987 | http://www.jrhokkaido.co.jp/ | n.a. |
| 68 | East Japan Railway Company | n.a. | n.a. | 01/04/1987 | http://www.jreast.co.jp/ | n.a. |

*Table 2.1* (*Continued*)

| | Cabinet Office (3) | No. of board members | No. of employees | Established | Website URL | Yearly salary of top executive (estimated millions Yen) |
|---|---|---|---|---|---|---|
| 69 | Central Japan Railway Company | n.a. | n.a. | 01/04/1987 | http://www.jrtokai.net/ | n.a. |
| 70 | West Japan Railway Company | n.a. | n.a. | 01/04/1987 | http://www.westjr.co.jp/ | n.a. |
| 71 | Shikoku Railway Company | 9 | 3 384 | 01/04/1987 | http://www.jr-shikoku.co.jp/ | 29.90 |
| 72 | Kyushu Railway Company | 14 | 10 719 | 01/04/1987 | http://www.jrkyushu.co.jp/ | n.a. |
| 73 | Japan Freight Railway Company | 12 | 8 726 | 01/04/1987 | http://www.jrfreight.co.jp/ | n.a. |
| 74 | Fund for the Promotion and Development of the Amami Islands (FPDAI) | n.a. | n.a. | n.a. | http://www2.ocn.ne.jp/~kikin/ | 14.70 |
| 75 | Japan National Tourist Organization (JNTO) | n.a. | n.a. | n.a. | http://www.jnto.go.jp/ | 23.30 |
| 76 | The Nippon Foundation | n.a. | n.a. | n.a. | http://www.nippon-foundation.or.jp/ | n.a. |
| 77 | Association for Housing for Workers of Japan | n.a. | n.a. | n.a. | http://www.kjk.go.jp/ | 14.14 |

|    |                                                              |      |      |            |                            |       |
|----|--------------------------------------------------------------|------|------|------------|----------------------------|-------|
|    | **Ministry of the Environment (2)**                          |      |      |            |                            |       |
| 78 | Japan Environment Corporation                                | 5    | 152  | 01/10/1965 | http://www. jec.go.jp/     | 28.26 |
| 79 | Association for the Prevention and Compensation of Health Damaged by Pollution | n.a. | n.a. | n.a.       | http://www. kouken.or.jp/  | 22.67 |

*Source*: Ministry of Public Management, Home Affairs, Posts and Telecommunications Website <http://www.soumu.go.jp/gyoukan/kanri/satei/siryou10.pdf>

*Table 2.2* Profit and loss balance sheet for special corporations, as at 31 March 2001 (in millions of yen)

|                                              | Current liabilities | Long-term liabilities | Reserve required by a special law | Total liabilities | Capital | Surplus (loss) | Other capital | Total capital |
|----------------------------------------------|---------------------|-----------------------|-----------------------------------|-------------------|---------|----------------|---------------|---------------|
| Water Resources Development Corporation      | 140                 | 46 167                | 0                                 | 46 308            | 23      | 0              | 0             | 492           |
| Japan Green Resources Corporation            | 80                  | 8 470                 | 0                                 | 8 550             | 6 758   | 89             | 0             | 6 848         |
| Japan National Oil Corporation               | 113                 | 23 154                | 228                               | 23 497            | 16 367  | 4 215          | 0             | 12 152        |
| Metal Mining Agency of Japan                 | 6                   | 466                   | 0.7                               | 474               | 237     | 7              | 39            | 269           |
| Electric Power Development Co.               | 3 017               | 19 241                | 3                                 | 22 262            | 706     | 553            | 0             | 1 306         |

*Table 2.2 (Continued)*

| | Current liabilities | Long-term liabilities | Reserve required by a special law | Total liabilities | Capital | Surplus (loss) | Other capital | Total capital |
|---|---|---|---|---|---|---|---|---|
| New Energy and Industrial Technology Development Organization (NEDO) | 763 | 1 168 | 0 | 1 934 | 4 698 | 2 071 | 191 | 2 819 |
| Japan Atomic Energy Research Institute | 255 | 4 | 0 | 260 | 18 815 | 15 327 | 0 | 3 427 |
| Japan Nuclear Cycle Development Institute | 192 | 517 | 0 | 709 | 29 215 | 22 466 | 0 | 6 769 |
| Japan Regional Development Corporation (JRCD) | 345 | 5 904 | 481 | 6 732 | 1 357 | 101 | 0 | 1 475 |
| The Okinawa Development Finance Corporation | 595 | 16 639 | 0 | 17 238 | 631 | 0 | 30 | 662 |
| Association for the Restoration of the Japanese Kurile Islands | 0.3 | 45 | 0 | 45 | 10 | 8 | 0 | 18 |
| Fund for the Promotion and Development of the Amami Islands (FPDAI) | 4 | 279 | 0 | 283 | 114 | 5 | 0 | 109 |

| | | | | | | | | |
|---|---|---|---|---|---|---|---|---|
| Japan Highway Corporation (JH) | 3 924 | 270 335 | 98 255 | 372 515 | 19 800 | 327 | 0 | 20 128 |
| Metropolitan Expressway Corporation (MEX) | 479 | 48 367 | 13 434 | 62 281 | 5 969 | 5 | 0 | 5 975 |
| Hanshin Expressway Corporation | 535 | 39 405 | 3 869 | 43 810 | 4 702 | 0 | 0 | 4 702 |
| Honshu–Shikoku Bridge Authority | 233 | 42 033 | 114 | 42 382 | 7 655 | 9 990 | 0 | 2 335 |
| Japan Railway Construction Corporation (JRCC) | 2 001 | 54 364 | 42 | 56 408 | 341 | 33 235 | 0 | 33 877 |
| New Tokyo International Airport Authority | 274 | 5 580 | 62 | 5 917 | 2 846 | 50 | 0 | 2 795 |
| Corporation for Advanced Transport & Technology (CATT) | 469 | 68 041 | 0 | 68 510 | 366 | 9 466 | 0 | 9 700 |
| Teito Rapid Transport Authority | 1 768 | 10 205 | 0 | 11 973 | 581 | 350 | 145 | 1 077 |
| Kansai International Airport Company Ltd | 1 079 | 10 718 | 0 | 11 797 | 5 920 | 1 729 | 0 | 4 191 |
| Urban Development Corporation | 11 383 | 155 272 | 0 | 169 166 | 689 | 355 | 0 | 6 524 |
| Association for Housing for Workers of Japan | 1 113 | 168 | 26 | 1 307 | 0 | 12 | 2 | 14 |
| Japan Environment Corporation | 50 | 4 074 | 0.04 | 4 126 | 156 | 0.1 | 41 | 197 |

*Table 2.2* *(Continued)*

| | Current liabilities | Long-term liabilities | Reserve required by a special law | Total liabilities | Capital | Surplus (loss) | Other capital | Total capital |
|---|---|---|---|---|---|---|---|---|
| Association for the Prevention and Compensation of Health Damaged by Pollution | 6 | 8 | 145 | 160 | 60 | 26 | 449 | 536 |
| Social Welfare and Medical Service Corporation | 1 384 | 27 747 | 0 | 29 131 | 2 925 | 9 | 0 | 2 933 |
| Government Pension Investment Fund | 2 544 | 359 731 | 0 | 362 276 | 10 754 | 21 556 | 0 | 10 443 |
| Postal Life Insurance Welfare Corporation | 9 352 | 268 549 | 0 | 277 903 | 4 422 | 448 | 0 | 3 974 |
| Social Insurance Medical Fee Payment Fund | 6 454 | 953 | 0 | 7 407 | 0 | 56 | 0 | 56 |
| Mutual Aid Association of Agriculture, Forestry and Fisheries Corporation Personnel | 21 | 1 064 | 20 113 | 21 187 | 0 | 15 | 0 | 15 |
| Fund for Farmers' Pension | 196 | 6 058 | 0 | 6 255 | 0 | 5 033 | 0 | 5 032 |
| Organization for Workers' Retirement Allowance Mutual Aid | 56 | 42 652 | 0 | 42 709 | 0 | 1 725 | 0 | 1 725 |

| | | | | | | | | |
|---|---|---|---|---|---|---|---|---|
| Agriculture and Livestock Industries Corporation (ALIC) | 737 | 19 | 1 641 | 2 403 | 166 | 433 | 3 633 | 4 233 |
| Labour Welfare Corporation | 449 | 353 | 0 | 803 | 7 230 | 2 522 | 0 | 4 708 |
| Employment and Human Resources Development Organization of Japan | 553 | 7 112 | 0 | 7 667 | 21 192 | 5 214 | 0 | 15 978 |
| Development Bank of Japan | 162 801 | 2 847 | 0 | 165 653 | 10 393 | 141 | 9 518 | 19 771 |
| Japan Bank for International Co-operation | 142 059 | 5 700 | 0 | 147 761 | 69 862 | 0 | 7 926 | 77 791 |
| The Shoko Chukin Bank (The Central Co-operative Bank for Commerce and Industry) | 30 513 | 102 832 | 0 | 134 043 | 4 939 | 901 | 244 | 6 085 |
| National Finance Corporation | 528 | 106 109 | 0 | 106 698 | 3 218 | 0 | 0 | 3 218 |
| Agriculture, Forestry and Fisheries Finance Corporation | 448 | 37 752 | 0 | 38 201 | 3 111 | 0 | 0 | 3 111 |
| Japan Small and Medium Enterprise Corporation | 700 | 85 954 | 238 | 88 551 | 35 531 | 7 797 | 1 928 | 29 664 |
| Japan Finance Corporation for Small Business | 619 | 72 270 | 0 | 72 892 | 4 109 | 0 | 0 | 4 109 |

*Table 2.2   (Continued)*

| | Current liabilities | Long-term liabilities | Reserve required by a special law | Total liabilities | Capital | Surplus (loss) | Other capital | Total capital |
|---|---|---|---|---|---|---|---|---|
| The Government Housing Loan Corporation | 7 728 | 766 509 | 0 | 774 240 | 1 662 | 0 | 1 543 | 3 206 |
| Japan Finance Corporation for Municipal Enterprises (JFM) | 228 002 | 8 743 | 12 786 | 249 533 | 166 | 0 | 0 | 166 |
| National Space Development Agency of Japan | 614 | 1 | 0 | 616 | 29 875 | 24 337 | 0 | 5 537 |
| Japan Science and Technology Corporation | 223 | 9 | 0 | 233 | 5 482 | 3 607 | 0 | 1 875 |
| Japan Consumer Information Centre | 4 | 3 | 0 | 8 | 94 | 35 | 0 | 59 |
| Institute of Physical and Chemical Research | 163 | 6 | 0 | 170 | 5 545 | 3 074 | 0 | 2 471 |
| The Japan Institute of Labour | 6 | 4 | 0 | 10 | 60 | 6 | 0 | 53 |
| The Promotion and Mutual Aid Corporation for Private Schools in Japan | 6 207 | 55 400 | 5 | 61 619 | 487 | 16 232 | 489 | 15 255 |

| | | | | | | | | |
|---|---|---|---|---|---|---|---|---|
| Japan Scholarship Foundation | 8 | 24 590 | 0 | 24 598 | 37 | 46 | 0 | 83 |
| Japan Arts Council | 35 | 54 | 0 | 90 | 3 894 | 532 | 111 | 4 538 |
| Japan Society for the Promotion of Science | 5 | 14 | 1 | 20 | 1 025 | 1 018 | 0 | 6 |
| The University of the Air | 71 | 101 | 0 | 173 | 239 | 85 | 0 | 153 |
| Association for the Welfare of the Mentally and Physically Disabled | 2 | 4 | 0 | 6 | 102 | 38 | 0 | 64 |
| Japan International Co-operation Agency | 325 | 62 | 0 | 387 | 1 326 | 50 | 0 | 1 275 |
| The Japan Foundation | 9 | 64 | 8 | 82 | 1 062 | 26 | 0 | 1 088 |
| Japan External Trade Organization (JETRO) | 48 | 60 | 0 | 109 | 1 035 | 213 | 3 | 1 251 |
| Japan National Tourist Organization (JNTO) | 7 | 3 | 0 | 11 | 13 | 4 | 0 | 18 |
| Japan Racing Association (JRA) | 505 | 289 | 0 | 794 | 49 | 10 800 | 0 | 10 850 |
| The National Association of Racing | 13 | 13 | 0 | 26 | 0 | 95 | 0 | 95 |
| Japan Keirin Association | 217 | 9 | 0 | 227 | 0 | 5 | 650 | 655 |

*Table 2.2* (*Continued*)

|  | Current liabilities | Long-term liabilities | Reserve required by a special law | Total liabilities | Capital | Surplus (loss) | Other capital | Total capital |
|---|---|---|---|---|---|---|---|---|
| Japan Auto Racing Association | 30 | 14 | 0 | 45 | 0 | 2 | 108 | 155 |
| The Nippon Foundation | 66 | 3 | 0 | 70 | 270 | 104 | 2 556 | 2 932 |
| National Stadium and School Health Centre of Japan | 31 | 186 | 50 | 270 | 453 | 32 | 0 | 530 |
| **Total for all special corporations** | 583 782 | 1 319 741 | 14 729 | 1 920 718 | 212 627 | 46 540 | 28 709 | 194 796 |

*Source*: Office of the Cabinet: Administrative Reform Promotion Office.

# 3

# The Bureaucracy: Origins of Power

## Defining the governing system

Political science tends to look at a democratic government in terms of a distinct division of power between the executive, the legislature and the judiciary branches. The legislature makes laws, the executive implements the laws, and the judiciary ensures that the laws are implemented and obeyed.

To Western observers, the source of power in Japan's post-war governing system can appear to be nebulous because, although the system hinges on an American-style constitution initiated by the Occupation Forces allied to a parliamentary system that resembles the United Kingdom's, there does not seem to be any clearly defined power base.

The Japanese describe their governing system as a 'ruling triad' of conservative politicians, elite bureaucrats, and leading businessmen (*sei kan zai*).[1] These institutions are bound together by elements inherent in the Japanese socio-political system,[2] resulting in a deep and abiding relationship. Karel van Wolferen coined the term 'the System'[3] to define this method of governing, which he believed was not controlled by a single group, nor was it led by an executive body that accepted accountability. Rather, Japan's government was based on an interaction of mechanisms that constituted a system that did not resemble Western governments. He contended that there was no central force, and that no institution had 'ultimate jurisdiction' over other institutions.[4]

On the other hand, Chalmers Johnson maintains that the bureaucracy rules:

Who governs is Japan's elite bureaucracy. The bureaucracy drafts virtually all laws, ordinances, regulations and licenses that govern society. It also has extensive powers of 'administrative guidance'[5] and is comparatively unrestrained in any way, both in theory and in practice by the judicial system. To find a comparative official elite in the United States, one would have to look at those who staffed the E-Ring of the Pentagon or the Central Intelligence Agency at the height of the Cold War.[6]

Johnson is not alone in his estimation. Many scholars judge Japan's government machine as being powered by the bureaucracy. Kent E. Calder calls METI and MOF, the chief architects' of Japan's expanding economic presence in global markets.[7]

In their recent book, *Japan's Policy Trap* (2002), Akio Mikuni and R. Taggart Murphy evaluate Japan's central government as possessing little real power, describing it as a 'weak confederation of ministries' acting as 'sovereign entities', each administering and acting for segments of society. In other words, the bureaucracy not only controls industrial sectors, but is also involved in other realms of Japanese society.

'The Fundamental Structure of the Government of Japan', the government's official explanation on the structure of government seems to indicate that the prime minister's office has substantial power:

> National administration is uniformly carried out by the Cabinet and the organizations under the Cabinet. The Cabinet, Ministries, Agencies and public corporations form one organization at the top of which exists the Cabinet. It is responsible for all activities of the State except legislative and judicial ones. Consequently, it is natural that the agencies and corporations which take care of national administration should be systematically organized under the Cabinet.[8]

This explanation contends that, among the powers that the Constitution gives the prime minister and his ministers are: 'to administer law faithfully, to conduct affairs of State, to manage foreign affairs, to conclude treaties, to administer the civil service, to prepare the budget and present it to the Diet'.

The official explanation also states that the prime minister appoints a minister to represent each ministry and they are assisted by the administrative vice-ministers from each ministry 'as a way to keep in order the affairs of the Ministry and to supervise the working of respective bureaus and divisions, attached agencies and local branches'.

The explanation suggests that the prime minister and his Cabinet are at the helm of government, but Mikuni and Murphy contend that there is little executive control. They credit Michisada Hirose, an editor at the *Asahi Shimbun*, one of Japan's major dailies, for describing the governing system as being controlled by the bureaucracy. Not only are the prime minister and his cabinet ministers subject to ministerial guidance but also politicians belonging to the LDP, who depend on government subsidies for their constituents, subsidies that Hirose claims total 30 per cent of the national budget.[9]

Mikuni's and Murphy's contentions are realistic. Although former Prime Minister Hashimoto's reform of the bureaucracy was intended to give the executive office more executive power, at the time of writing, there has yet to be a noticeable change in the balance of power as is seen in Koizumi's struggle to reform the ministries' special corporations.

Tracing elite rule back a thousand years to when an aristocracy governed Japan,[10] Mikuni and Murphy state that elite bureaucrats are today's policy-makers, who operate independently of legal sanctions, thus giving them unlimited power.[11] Indeed, until 1867 and the overthrow of a military regime that had ruled Japan since 1603 (known as the Tokugawa period), marking the end of feudalism, the Japanese had relied consistently on an emperor or a military regime to lead them. Even after the fall of the military, a new power took its place – namely, a bureaucracy.

Japan's current governing system is not entirely a product of post-war Japan. The seeds of the modern bureaucracy were sown at the beginning of the Meiji Restoration in 1868. The source of bureaucratic power originated during the Meiji period (1868–1914), when the government endowed the bureaucracy with the authority to convert a feudal Japan into an industrialized country. The ties with big business began at the end of the nineteenth century, when the government with the support of the large family-owned combines converted a technologically backward nation into an industrialized economy, which by the 1920s was to rival the already industrialized Western powers.

## The Meiji Restoration, the birth of the modern bureaucracy and the roots of the 'ruling triad': the source of bureaucratic power

When the American Commodore Matthew C. Perry arrived unannounced at the port of Uraga in 1853, demanding on behalf of the United States that the *shogun* (military leader) open his country to foreign trade, the Japanese were taken completely by surprise. Several hundred years of xenophobic policies by the military government had isolated the population from contact with foreigners, and until Perry's sudden appearance with his armada of 'black ships' the Japanese had assumed that they were impervious to invasion. The government, recognizing that Japan was unable to defend itself against a Western military power, signed a trade agreement the following year. Other trade agreements with Great Britain, France and Russia were signed within the next few years.

Japan was already experiencing civil unrest before Perry's arrival. After the American ambassador to Japan set foot on Japanese soil, followed by diplomats from Great Britain and France in 1857, ten years of turmoil ensued. The realization that the military regime was unprepared to deal with foreign aggression coupled with the fear of occupation by a Western power (as was its neighbour China) was the decisive factor in the overthrow of the military and the beginning of land reform.

Aristocrats were at the helm when the Meiji government was engineered, only this time they were joined by elite *samurai* from clans in Western Japan, retainers who had served simultaneously as administrators of their lords' lands and soldiers in their lords' armies in times of strife. During the Tokugawa period, the social order was rigid, with the *samurai* at the top of the social hierarchy, followed by farmers, artisans and merchants. *Samurai* also filled a number of administrative posts in local government depending on their rank.[12] Some of them and their offspring became administrators in the Meiji government.

Restoring the Imperial Family as constitutional monarchs, the group of aristocrats and elite *samurai* formed a Cabinet. In 1889 they composed a constitution resembling Prussia's, and established a parliament with a House of Peers and a House of Representatives. Among the leading statesmen were Takanori Saigo, Shigenobu Okuma and Toshimichi Okubo.[13] Okubo and his colleagues were keenly aware that, compared to the Western industrialized nations, Japan was conspicuously behind in most technologies. If the Japanese were to protect national interests they would have to become as powerful both economically and militarily.

The Cabinet formed agencies to implement land reform and to guide the country through the process of industrialization. Okubo became the head of the Home Office, Japan's first ministry to be established, which managed the land reform. He is credited by many Japanese with giving the bureaucracy extraordinary powers to administrate. The ministries of Foreign Affairs, Finance, Army–Navy, Justice, Education, Agriculture and Commerce were also established. The provinces were dependent on administrators posted from central government. Some of the staff had been former *samurai*. In 1886, the Meiji government founded Tokyo Imperial University for the purpose of training civil servants.[14]

The constitution provided the bureaucracy with power and prestige.[15] The Japanese people regarded elite civil servants in the same way they had related to the *shogun* – with awe, respect and trepidation, and the source of power of elite civil servants can be traced to this time.

### The bureaucracy, big business and the industrialization of Japan: 1890–1914

The government could be described as pluralistic because authority was dispersed among various administering bodies headed by elite officials.[16]

The slogan of the Meiji Period was 'Prosperous Country, Strong Country, Strong Military'. The primary purpose of government policy was to advance Japan's economic welfare.[17] To achieve the government's objective, the ministries, together with the family-owned combines (henceforth referred to as *zaibastu*)[18] imported technologies from the Western industrialized nations such as Germany, the United States and the United Kingdom. Technical support was also imported. Although there were a number of foreign technicians working for the feudal lords before 1868, after the Meiji Restoration there was an influx of American, British, French and Dutch workers, who were hired by the government to serve as railroad and marine engineers, pilots, financial and legal consultants, educators, military instructors and agricultural experts.[19] Japanese citizens were sent abroad to study engineering, mining, commerce and agriculture.

The early Meiji economy was supported by rice cultivation and light industries such as cotton and silk yarn spinning and small tool production. The textile industry experienced rapid development. By 1897, exports exceeded imports as Japan became entirely self-sufficient in cotton textiles. By 1907 large companies had joined to form textile oligopolies, driving British yarn from the domestic market.[20]

Japan's industrial output grew rapidly before the Sino-Japanese War in 1894, but afterwards there was a period of stagnation caused partially by the Boxer Rebellion in 1900, when exports to China came to a halt. However, the government encouraged the development of heavy industries such as iron, steel and shipbuilding through subsidies to shipyards and to merchants who purchased the ships for trade.

The Ministry of Agriculture and Commerce (MAC) was a major player in guiding industrial development, managing and regulating the development of the machinery, shipbuilding and heavy industries. MAC administrated the construction of the first hydropower station in 1907, by the Tokyo Electric Light Co., as well as subsequent power stations. The new supply of electric power increased industrial output and encouraged new businesses.

The *zaibatsu* co-operated closely with the ministries in the industrial development of Japan with large capital investment. They were involved in merchant banking, trade and manufacturing. Sumitomo and Mitsui were merchant companies during the Tokugawa period. Sumitomo originally engaged in copper mining and currency exchange (the currency used in the Kansai region was silver while the currency in the Kanto area was gold). Mitsui engaged in the wholesale business and in currency exchange. Mitsubishi began operations during the Meiji Period in foreign commerce, shipbuilding and heavy industries. And many small and medium-sized businesses started up, often serving as suppliers to the *zaibatsu*, a relationship that ripened during the Second World War.

In 1890, the mass production of steel commenced at the Osaka Armoury after the installation of Japan's first open-hearth furnace.

Initially, Japanese production was insignificant – in 1894 steel production amounted to no more than 1,000 tons and Japan had to
import 90,000 tons. To accelerate production, the government built
a steel mill, creating the Yawata Company. Sumitomo Steel, Kobe
Steel (the steel division of Kawasaki Shipbuilding Co.) and Nippon
Steel Pipe Co. began production consecutively. By 1914, the new
steel companies succeeded in producing for domestic use 44 per cent
of rolled steel and 64 per cent of pig iron.[21]

### The bureaucracy, big business and the industrialization of Japan: 1914–28

The Emperor Meiji died in 1914. During his successor Emperor
Taisho's reign (1914–26) great advances were seen in the smoke stack
industries such as coal, steel and shipbuilding. The co-operation
between the *zaibatsu* and the ministries remained constant.

Japan did not enter the First World War and her country's industries benefited significantly through supplying the Western powers'
military with ships, coal and steel. Nevertheless, the end of the
war marked the beginning of a rapid decline in orders for ships. As
surpluses increased, Japan slipped to a ranking of ninth place among
the shipbuilding nations. Reacting to recessive markets, shipbuilders
invested heavily in developing other technologies – to improve ship's
engines, and to diversify into general machinery, aircraft and motor
vehicles. For example, Izuzu Motors Co. was the new motor vehicle
division of the Ishikawa Shipbuilding Co. and Mitsubishi Heavy
Industries Co. was the new division of Mitsubishi Shipbuilding Co.[22]

Although by 1919, Japan's economy was booming because of
post-war construction activities, expanded exports and new business
start-ups, a stock market crash on 15 March 1920 triggered a panic.
Inventories of raw silk, cotton textiles and rice piled up and businesses
went bankrupt. The government and the Bank of Japan reacted by
supplying substantial funds to banks to provide loans to key industries and to prop up the stock market. Despite these measures Japan's
economy suffered a stunning blow when the Yokohama–Tokyo region
was hit by the Great Kano Earthquake of September 1923. Infrastructure was heavily damaged and business transactions were suspended.
In addition, Japan's trade deficit escalated because of the imports of
massive quantities of goods for reconstruction.

In 1925, to deal with mounting economic problems, MAC separated into two agencies, the Ministry of Agriculture and Forestry, and the Ministry of Commerce and Industry (MCI). MCI established the Commerce and Industry Deliberation Council, an organization whose members represented private industry. With the co-operation of the Council, MCI planned policy to protect industry from the effects of the depression. The organization was the predecessor of the current Industrial Structure Council and, according to Clyde V. Prestowitz, Jr, the concept of 'industrial rationalization' developed during that time.[23] MCI expanded its control over industry, writing laws that allowed the ministry to form cartels, the laws passed by a supportive Diet. Prestowitz claims that these laws laid the foundation for ministerial use of the policy instrument 'administrative guidance'.[24]

The Japanese suffered yet another crisis when government was unable to cover the payments of the massive quake disaster bill. In mid-April, 1927, banks closed for several days sending the country into what is known as the Panic of 1927.

Nonetheless, despite the country's economic turbulence, Japan received worldwide recognition as a fully industrialized nation by 1928.

### The bureaucracy and big business: the Second World War

The advent of the war brought new powers to the economic ministries, MCI and the Ministry of Finance (MOF) as well as a closer alliance with the *zaibatsu*, which produced armaments and military supplies. MCI managed and regulated industry as a whole, as well as munitions production, changing its name in 1942 to the Ministry of Munitions. Since the *zaibatsu* engaged in all kinds of manufacturing and finance, a close partnership was an inevitable result of the all-out effort to win the war in the Pacific.

In 1944, the 'System of Financial Institutions Authorized to Finance Munitions Companies' was established, the bill giving the government the authority to order private banks to fund munitions manufacturers thus ensuring a steady supply of armaments. Government banks provided funds to the private banks that were run by the *zaibatsu*. Each bank was assigned to one munitions firm. Takafusa Nakamura maintains that the relationship between government and private banks and big business continued during the post-war reconstruction, resulting in the formation of the giant financial groups or *keiretsu*.[25]

A *keiretsu* is a group of large companies that centre on a single bank, have cross shareholdings and directors in common. The group sub-contracts to small and medium-sized businesses for parts and services, many of which receive investment from the *keiretsu*. Such well-known *keiretsu* as Mitsubishi, Mitsui, and Sumitomo are involved in businesses that they engaged in before the war, such as international trade, mining, retail banking and ship building.

The two economic ministries, MITI and MOF, continued to plan and implement Japan's monetary and industrial policy through their relationship with big business.

1869. land reform China.

Japan model began after World War 2

Taiwan & Korea followed by after.

下尺扣州, 台湾和韩阳

# 4

# The Power of the Bureaucracy:
# The Continuing Saga

*Summarises Japan's post-war governance system set up by the supreme Command of the Allied Power, to show how America's post-war policies continued to give Japan's bureaucracy extraordinary power to administrate the country's economy.*

The period 1945 to 1952 is commonly referred to as the Allied Occupation. The occupying countries were the United States, Great Britain and Australia. Great Britain and Australia sent few troops compared to those from the United States, which commandeered the Occupation under the leadership of General Douglas MacArthur, the Supreme Commander of the Allied Powers (SCAP). The objectives of the Occupation were three-fold: Japan's demilitarization and democratization; the purging of war criminals; and Japan's economic resuscitation.[1] SCAP issued orders for the composition of a liberal constitution that included the right of women to vote, the right of labour unions to organize and the liberalization of the educational system. The Socialist and Communist parties that had been banned during the war were allowed to reorganize.

The Occupation was scheduled to end by 1948 with a democratic and liberal governing system in place. However, Communist-backed labour strikes in 1947 and 1948, accompanied by demonstrations by Communist sympathizers, the beginning of the Cold War with the Soviet Union and the Korean War in 1950 caused SCAP to reverse some of the reforms. Reacting to the perceived danger of Communist expansion in East Asia, the United States was determined to cultivate a strong and conservative ally in the Pacific where it could base its military forces and hardware. The San Francisco Peace Treaty signed in October 1950 formalized the alliance. SCAP, in an effort to promote swift economic recovery, reinstated many of the pre-war bureaucrats and essentially the same ministries continued to manage Japan's economy. Communist sympathizers were purged and the

United States backed a conservative coalition party in the Diet. The Liberal Democratic Party resulted from this policy, coming to power in 1955. ( *LDP* ) —> henceforth.

## Japan's post-war 'ruling triad': the Liberal Democratic Party (*sei*), big business (*zai*) and the bureaucracy (*kan*)

### The Liberal Democratic Party (*sei*)

The Liberal Democratic Party (LDP) dominated Japanese politics until 1993 when Hosokawa became prime minister. The period is known as the '1955 political system'.[2] The LDP returned to power in 1996.

The party supported the ministries' policies consistently, giving bureaucrats independence to implement policies at will. The MCI and the Board of Trade were merged to form the Ministry of International Trade and Industry (MITI) in 1949, and elite officials benefited from the party's co-operation, experiencing tremendous freedom.[3]

In most Western countries, no single political party has been in power long enough to give bureaucrats the consistent support to draft laws and implement policies, nor are there democratic societies where the ministries can operate unfettered by legal sanction as they operate in Japan. There are two key reasons for this unwavering political support, both related to the network of civil servants throughout Japan's social political system. The first is that bureaucrats will seek political office in both national and local government Diets on the LDP ticket.[4] The second reason is that the LDP receives substantial support from special interest groups represented by the ministries *vis-à-vis* associations and federations.

Big business and business federations make large contributions to the LDP coffers. The LDP gets votes and large donations from traditional support groups such as small local businesses and businesses engaged in construction, transportation and telecommunications in exchange for contracts for public works projects. A recent example of this kind of patronage is the allocation of the stimulus packages released since 1992. Of the US$86 billion fiscal stimulus package released in August 1992, US$69 billion went to public works and US$17 billion to small business and capital investment.[5]

The money from these packages can be distributed through special corporations to local governments for construction contracts or for loans to small and medium-sized businesses. In 1989, Kent E. Calder wrote that special corporations supplied the overwhelming number of positions for former bureaucrats, many of the corporations being involved in the aid of small businesses.[6] METI (MITI) oversees the small and medium-sized business sector, which constitutes 99 per cent of all business activity in Japan and employs approximately 78 per cent of the workforce.

MITI established special corporations in the 1950s to provide loans and other services to independent small and medium-sized businesses.[7] Two of these corporations are still operating. The Japan Finance Corporation for Small Businesses (JFS) has ¥410.9 billion in capital resources and is a primary lender to small businesses, offering long-term loans at interest rates that are lower than private financial institutions. FILP funds the JFS budget. As of 31 March 2001 there were 1,751 employees and sixty offices throughout Japan. There is also a branch office located in the offices of JETRO in New York City and one in Kuala Lumpur.[8]

The Japan Small and Medium Enterprise Agency (JAMEC) is a consolidation of the Small Business Credit Insurance Corporation, Japan Small Business Corporation and the Textile Industry Restructuring Agency.[9] The capital resource is ¥3.5 trillion emanating from FILP. JAMEC helps small businesses to upgrade operations by providing finance, but business owners must apply through their local government authority for the loans, which, in turn, requests the loans from the JAMEC. The JAMEC distributes the money to local government, which then passes it on to applicants.

The JAMEC also engages in joint business ventures and in the 'collective establishment of factories and stores, etc.' There is the Mutual Relief System for Small Scale Enterprises, with 2 million subscribers (funds total ¥7.4 trillion), and the Mutual Relief System for the Prevention of Bankruptcies in SMEs, with 410,000 subscribers and loans totalling ¥343 billion. There are 948 employees and nineteen domestic offices. The JAMEC also operates three overseas offices, one at JETRO New York, one at JETRO Bangkok and one at JETRO Shanghai.

With these kinds of government subsidies in hand it is not surprising that small-business owners support the political party that supports the ministries they rely on heavily.

## Big business (*zai*)

One of the punitive measures ordered by SCAP was the dismantling of the *zaibatsu*. The *zaibatsu* that were operating before the Second World War were Sumitomo, Mitsui, Mitsubishi and Yasuda. The *zaibatsu* that were formed during the war through close co-operation with the military were Nissan, Asano, Okura, Nomura Nakajima and Furukawa. SCAP first dissolved the holding companies, so that the family owners no longer held the controlling interest. The 'economic purge' of the executives, who had directed the companies during the war, was delayed until January 1947, when ultimately 1,500 executives retired. The Mitsubishi and Mitsui trading companies were dismantled in July 1947.[10] Many other companies were earmarked for liquidation, but the Cold War and the fear of Communist expansion in the Pacific convinced SCAP to reverse its initial stand and follow a more lenient course, so that the large combines could join with the ministries, namely MITI and MOF, to rebuild Japan's economy.

The signing of the San Francisco Peace Treaty in 1950 saw the abandonment of the reform that forbade *zaibatsu* families from owning shares in their own firms. Cross-share holding between firms was also allowed. Even though four of the *zaibatsu* regrouped after the Occupation, the initial modification of the punitive reforms perpetuated the continued close alliance between the bureaucracy and big business. The groups became known as *keiretsu* (discussed in Chapter 3).

## The bureaucracy (*kan*)

Johnson contends that Japan's post-war bureaucracy was merely a continuation of the powerful pre-war bureaucracy, because of SCAP's objectives in the Pacific. He claims that while SCAP purged the wartime government officials, they reinstated former ministry officials to manage Japan's economic and industrial recovery, thereby preserving Japan's pre-war institutions and economic system.[11]

On the other hand, Seiichiro Yonekura, who wrote about the role that industrial associations have played in the regulation of industry, claims that because wartime controls had failed and Japan's governing system had been democratized 'the continuity in experience of wartime into the post-war periods of MITI bureaucrats does not follow a direct, unbroken course'. He suggests that Johnson used the continuity of staff in the post-war bureaucracy to promote his theory. Yonekura feels that the continuity is not as evident in the economic system as it is in the experiences of the bureaucrats who managed industry during the war and who understood the 'limitations' of such controls and the meaning of 'withholding controls'.[12]

Yonekura gives a number of examples pointing to this continuity of wartime elite MCI officials who became members of MITI, the consolidation of MCI and the Board of Trade in 1949. Takayuki Yamamoto worked in the general affairs division of MCI and was in charge of product expansion. After the war he took the position of administrative vice-minister when MITI was established.

Yonekura's other examples are Nobusuke Kishi and Etsuburo Shina. In 1942, Kishi was Minister of Commerce and Industry. After the war he became Prime Minister in 1957, retiring in 1961. Etsusaburo Shina was the vice-minister of MCI in 1942, and was appointed Minister of International Trade and Industry in 1961.[13]

The nature of bureaucratic rule and the character of the bureaucracy remained intact because the officials who planned Japan's post-war industrial recovery were former officers of MCI. Since the top officials had been former colleagues, they had a close relationship with each other and a strong loyalty to their former ministry. Endowed by SCAP with extraordinary powers they used their prior experiences to forge Japan's industrial policies during the country's period of rapid economic growth.

SCAP staff's ignorance of the Japanese language and social system forced them to rely on existing institutions, namely the bureaucracy, to implement reform policies. After SCAP's exit from Japan these institutions continued to operate, possessing more power than they had before the war.[14]

MOF and MITI's post-war economic and industrial policies are credited with Japan's post-war rapid industrial growth (1950–73). MITI officials operated unfettered by legal sanctions, planning a protectionist industrial policy[15] that promoted exports and capital investment. The ministry first focused attention on reviving the smoke-stack industries, coal and steel, in order to nurture motor vehicle production and the energy-intensive industries such as petrochemicals, shipbuilding and aluminum production. The 1949 Foreign Exchange Law gave MITI the right to control foreign exchange until 1964. MITI controlled licensing, favouring Japanese companies. MITI also controlled the distribution of fossil fuels to industry, accommodating the industries deemed to be crucial to national interests. MITI established special corporations such as the Industrial Bank of Japan, the Long-Term Trust Bank and the Japan Import–Export Bank, setting up a system through which the banks could invest capital in industries, which encouraged long-term corporate planning.

By 1953, Japan's production, national income and consumption had returned to pre-war levels and by 1973 Japan had become the world's third largest economy (following the United States and Russia), its growth rate accelerating to 10 per cent annually. Nevertheless, there is no hard quantitative evidence that defines the extent to which industrial policy in fact contributed.[16] Certainly, MITI officials' efforts were aided by a number of factors:

  (i)    the fixed rate of exchange of ¥360 per dollar in 1849, undervaluing the yen so that Japanese exports could have easier access to world markets;

  (ii)   the SCAP purge of Communist sympathizers and the quelling of labour strikes in order to ensure a stable environment for industrial growth;

 (iii)   anti-monopoly legislation revised to allow MITI to form depression and rationalization cartels, to control retail pricing and to sanction inter-corporate share holdings;

  (iv)  access to cheap technologies;

  (v)   the Tokyo Olympics that marked a spurt in industrial development as the Japanese prepared for the influx of foreign tourists;

  (vi)  consistent support for policy from both the Diet and business;

 (vii)  the successful efforts to internationalize by large trading firms such as Mitsubishi, Mitsui, and Marubeni, and by such corporations as Sony, Honda, Matsushita and Kyocera;

(viii)  America's willingness to open markets to the surge of Japanese exports in order to maintain a strong alliance in the Pacific;

  (ix)  the industriousness of the Japanese themselves and their willingness to follow the encouragement by MITI and MOF to save their earnings.

From the early 1950s onwards MITI, together with the other ministries, established special corporations and other types of public corporation as well as industrial federations. Even though these organizations served to promote economic revitalization they also began serving as informal ministerial control mechanisms over respective industrial sectors.

The oil shock of December 1973 ended Japan's rapid economic growth abruptly. MITI officials, who had focused on long-term planning for the energy-intensive industries since the 1950s, were taken totally unaware. Industries such as steel, chemicals, paper, aluminum and petrochemicals suffered structural problems. The policies were scrapped and MITI targeted the development of new industries such as those related to information systems. However, the industrial policy instruments that had been at MITI's disposal during Japan's period of rapid economic growth had decreased, giving MITI less control over industry.[17] MITI had relinquished control over foreign exchange by 1964, and cheap technologies were no longer useful to the maturing industries. Nevertheless, despite the economic environment and the need for a change in policy in order to open markets to foreign imports and foreign investment, which would stimulate domestic manufacturers to create innovative strategies to compete, MITI continued its protectionist policies, forming cartels to protect production and prices, and protect markets. Japan's economy remained entrenched in the exportation of manufactured goods.

Even though the kit of policy instruments had decreased, the ministries were able to secure co-operation from companies in their administrative jurisdiction through the extensive network of bureaucrats and former bureaucrats throughout the socio-political system, and the policy instrument, 'administrative guidance' (discussed in the following chapter), helped to persuade companies to comply with regulations.

Koji Matsumoto was serving in MITI when he wrote *The Rise of the Japanese Corporate System* in 1983.[18] Although he added a disclaimer that his opinions did not reflect those of his ministry, his book should be viewed as an officially approved account because the English version, printed in 1991 and reprinted in 1993, was distributed to American opinion leaders through one of MITI's special corporations, the Japan External Trade Organization. The book received high praise in reviews by the *Financial Times* and by Chalmers Johnson.

Matsumoto reassured readers that, by and large, MITI's duties did not interfere with corporate operations, and that the government's role was small in comparison with the role of the individual. He also denied that Japan's economy was planned or controlled, using as a benchmark the small number of staff in four of MITI's divisions. According to Matsumoto, in 1989 there were eleven staff in vehicle manufacturing, thirteen in computers (electronic policy), and thirteen in iron and steel manufacturing.

Matsumoto did not mention that beside the use of officials, MITI, as well as the other ministries, use other means to control industry such as through *amakudari* and through ministry officials posted as presidents of industrial associations and special corporations. Members of industrial associations and federations will acquiesce to guidance by elite officials posted as directors, and if they are reluctant to follow guidance they are pressured to comply by the other members. Kozo Yamamura agreed:

> Many formal and informal institutions, created and maintained in previous decades to actively aid the economy in 'catching-up' with and overtaking the Western industrialized economies, are still in place and continue to shape the behavior of all political and economic sectors.[19]

MITI's numerous industrial associations include the Japan Automobile Association, Japan Auto Parts Association, Japan Electrical Manufacturers Association, Inc., Electronic Industries Association of Japan, and Japan Information Processing Development Centre.

Regardless of the decrease in policy instruments, the ministries still maintained control and the power to act according to their own standards.

## The Japanese opinions of their bureaucracy

Prior to the bursting of the 'bubble economy', the Japanese in general regarded their elite civil servants as the cream of society. They enjoyed reading novels about elite civil servants, which portrayed them as highly intelligent, dedicated to their duties, loyal to their country and untainted by scandal. The general populace of Japan, who remained fairly isolated from politics, viewed the ministries as a world unto themselves, ivory towers of sorts. After all, the ministries' policies and guidance had created an economy that was second only to that of the United States. On the other hand, they viewed politicians as being untrustworthy and subject to influence by special interest groups. However, a profound interest in the internal politics and operations of the ministries began in the early 1990s, when a slew of scandals hit the ministries. The Recruit Scandal and the collapse of seven housing loan companies (*jusen*) started things off.[20] MOC officials were charged with colluding with politicians over contracts for public works, leading to the arrest of the governors of Ibaraki and Miyagi prefectures. MOF officials were charged with accepting favours in the form of lavish entertainment and bribes from the sectors they regulated, and tipping off banks about imminent government accounting audits. Also, in spite of MOF's pledge that no bank would ever fail, five large institutions collapsed.[21]

Members of the New Japan Party and Pioneer Party moved not only to reform the ministries but also to strengthen their position by pulling more officials into the political fold. Other tactics were used as well. In December 1993, Hiroshi Kumagai, the Minister of Commerce, Trade and Industry in Hosokawa's Cabinet, demanded the resignation of Masahisa Naito, the director-general of the Industrial Policy Bureau in MITI, and designated for the top post of administrative vice-minister of MITI. Kumagai himself had been a MITI official until he resigned in 1976 as director-general of the Small and Medium Enterprise Agency to run for political office on the LDP ticket. He won a seat in the Upper House of the National Diet in 1977 and then took a seat in the Lower House in 1983. In 1991 he served for one year as the parliamentary vice-minister of the Economic Planning Agency before assuming several high-ranking positions in the LDP. He was one of the founders of the New Japan Party. After serving in Hosokawa's Cabinet he served in 1994 as minister of state in former Prime Minister Hata's Cabinet. He later moved to the Democratic Party of Japan (DPJ) where he served as Secretary. After a power struggle with the head of the DPJ, Nato Kan, he defected along with three of his colleagues in December 2002 and formed the New Conservative Party, where at the time of writing, he serves as president.

While Kumagai was in MITI, his relationship with Naito is said to have been turbulent. Kumagai's reason for demanding Naito's resignation was that he had arranged a promotion in MITI for the son of his close friend,Yuji Tanahashi, a former MITI administrative vice-minister (retired in 1991).[22] Yasufumi had entered MITI in 1987. The promotion was intended to improve his image and thus his chances of winning a seat in the Diet when he entered the election as an LDP candidate from Gifu prefecture, a seat that his grandfather, a former governor of Gifu, had occupied for many years. Despite his new image, however, Yasufumi lost the race.

The incident rocked the halls of MITI. It was only the second time in the history of the ministry that a high-ranking official was dismissed (the first was in 1952). The Japanese media reported that Kumagai wanted to stop 'favoritism' in the ministries, using Naito as an example. Naito's dismissal was also related to the power struggle between factions within MITI and between the LDP and the Japan New Party.

Naito visited Kumagai's office on 16 December 1993. Kumagai told him that he cast darkness over the ministry. Naito's subordinates objected to politicians interfering in MITI's affairs and were opposed to his resignation but to no avail. When Naito visited Kumagai once again three days later at shortly after 10am, Kumagai told him that he could resign 'this month or next month, the process has begun'.[23] Hideaki Kumano, administrative-vice minister, and the head of MITI, was responsible for the dismissal. Although he was against Naito's resignation, in order to keep the peace, he pleaded with Naito to resign quietly. Naito refused but agreed to accept a dismissal. Kumano[24] had no choice but to dismiss him. Kumano offered his own resignation and left the ministry the following June.

After leaving MITI in April 1994 Naito moved to Georgetown University in Washington, DC to serve as the Marks & Murase[25] Professor, participating in the Asia Law and Policy Studies (ALPS) program.[26] He was reinstated in MITI in June as an 'adviser'.[27]

The incident is covered in detail by the editorial staff of *Nikkei Keizai Shimbun* for their book *The Bureaucracy: A Creaking Giant Power (Kanryo Kyodai Kenryoku)* published in 1994 at the height of the political reform movement. The book is a compilation of a series of articles that appeared daily on the front page of the newspaper earlier that year and which examined the relationship between the bureaucracy and the Diet as well as the power of the bureaucracy itself. It explained why bureaucrats were more influential than politicians in Japan's governing system, and why the Japanese did not believe that politicians could plan effective legislation, and that there was no real leadership in the Diet. The reasons given for their lack of confidence were: (i)) politicians were subservient to the whims of special interest groups; (ii)) there was ongoing friction between political factions; and (iii) politicians did not have the expertise or experience to plan effective policies because bureaucrats had been given the power to draft laws since the Meiji period.

The interviews with politicians and bureaucrats carried in the book illustrated the ministries' struggle to retain power during that time. The foreword began with the contention of a former MOF administrative vice-minister that elite bureaucrats were motivated by their belief in democracy. His convictions reflect the mind-set of bureaucrats who served with him during Japan's post-war period of economic rapid growth. The book also gives the views of young officials in the MOF and MITI, who seemed to be more aware that their ministries must become more egalitarian and that the relationship between the bureaucracy and politicians should be made more transparent.

Among the bureaucrats interviewed was Masahisa Naito who had spoken to *Nikkei* staff before his dismissal. When he asserted that bureaucrats operate independently of politicians he was asked if he thought that bureaucrats could work together with politicians to forge policy. Naito replied that it might prove feasible if politicians could plan strategies and the bureaucrats did the legwork, implying that administrators knew more about managing industry and economics than did politicians. He lamented that, although bureaucrats are the servants of their country, regrettably they become isolated from society and forget their mission.

Naito contended that the multitude of rules and regulations did not serve MITI by controlling industry but rather the trust between bureaucrats and private businesses facilitated the implementation of policy. Naito did not speak of the ways that the industrial federations, associations and special corporations helped MITI and the other ministries to persuade businesses to follow policies.

Hideaki Kumano was also interviewed before he resigned from MITI. He opposed the downsizing of MITI, taking exception to the interviewer calling MITI the 'number two' Ministry of Finance (*dainiji okurasho*), an insinuation that MITI was taking over MOF's territory[28] by executing duties that usually fell within MOF's jurisdiction.

Susumu Takahashi, a former administrative vice-minister in the Ministry of Construction, was interviewed about his views on *amakudari*. Takahashi admitted that there was an alliance between politicians and the MOC, and that there was indeed a relationship between the ministries and industry. However, he emphasized that denying bureaucrats post-retirement positions in industry was unrealistic, because bureaucrats had to retire earlier than corporate executives and they needed supplementary income. He was disturbed that elite officials, who are commonly referred to by the press as 'Old Boys' or 'OBs', received benefits from the civil service while they were working in post-retirement positions. Takashashi, who became the president of the Government Housing Loan Corporation in 1990 after he retired from MOC, claimed that the number of positions in special corporations was limited. He omitted to mention the number of positions available in subsidiaries of special corporations or in other institutions connected to the ministries.[29]

The results of a public survey conducted by *Nikkei Shimbun* in 1993, regarding how Japanese people felt about their bureaucracy, is included in the book. A good percentage of people questioned revealed their discontent with elite civil servants, reflecting their reaction to the disclosures of scandals involving the ministries. The perception of bureaucrats was: (i) they had a strong elitist mentality; (ii) they were irresponsible; and (iii) they were clever and shrewd. Twenty-two per cent answered that bureaucrats were cold and uncaring. Only 3 per cent believed that bureaucrats should be entrusted to plan policy independently, and an overwhelming 70 per cent agreed that bureaucrats should join forces with politicians to plan policy.

The newspaper conducted another survey at the end of October 1993 of 200 bureaucrats on their views of the governing system. 147 officers answered questions ranging from *amakudari* to devolution. Asked whether they would want their children to work for the ministries, although 44 per cent answered yes, 52 per cent answered that they could not positively promote working for the bureaucracy. Fifty-two per cent of respondents were over the age of fifty while 19 per cent of the respondents were in their twenties.

The question concerning *amakudari* brought some surprising answers; 45 per cent answered that the system opened a pipeline between business and the ministries. Only 22 per cent felt that *amakudari* was necessary because salaries were insufficient. Forty per cent of the bureaucrats, who were in their twenties, answered that the system should be discontinued while only 8 per cent among the over-fifty group of bureaucrats were for abolishing *amakudari*. The majority of them wanted to work after their retirement.

The questions about devolutions brought negative answers concerning the ability of local government to plan policies. The respondents insisted that the national ministries must always bear the responsibility of governing the regions.

As for the loosening of regulations and opening of Japan's markets, 63 per cent of the respondents in their twenties wanted deregulation. Fifty per cent of the respondents in their fifties were also for more deregulation.

The survey also asked bureaucrats which agencies they thought were no longer necessary or would no longer be necessary in the future. The Hokkaido Development Agency took first place. The reasons given were that the period of development in Hokkaido had passed and that the agency was ineffective. Among the ministries, MITI took first place. Although the respondents acknowledged that the ministry had done good work during the period of rapid growth, they felt that it lacked a clear vision and was now groping for an industrial policy, which would assist Japanese businesses internationalize. Also, there was criticism about MITI's tug of war with the Ministry of Transportation and the Ministry of Posts and Telecommunications over their administrative jurisdiction of the transportation and high-tech industries and information networks.

The *Mainichi Shimbun* also conducted a similar survey in 1993 December[30] but also included the general public in the survey as well. Although 77 per cent of the subjects questioned credited bureaucrats with Japan's rapid economic growth, 41 per cent of the subjects regarded bureaucrats in the 1990s as being greedy for power. Thirty-one per cent answered that bureaucrats worked for the benefit of their ministries, but only 18 per cent felt that bureaucrats worked for the good of their industrial sectors. A mere 3 per cent felt that bureaucrats were hardworking, and only 3 per cent considered bureaucrats to be honest and sincere.

Of the people surveyed, 60 per cent wanted *amakudari* abolished while only 12 per cent wanted the system maintained; 38 per cent wanted the system abolished for political office and 43 per cent of the people polled wanted the companies that hired bureaucrats subjected to strict regulations.

## The bureaucracy: power maintained

On 6 January 2001 the ministries formally regrouped as part of the reform of government operations. Some agencies were also included in the mergers. The Ministry of Home Affairs merged with the Ministry of Management and Coordination and the Ministry of Posts and Telecommunications[31] to form the Ministry of Public Management, Home Affairs, Posts and Telecommunications.[32] The Ministry of Education, which had the largest number of public corporations at 1,811, joined with the Science and Technology Agency to form the Ministry of Education, Culture, Sports, Science and Technology.[33] The Ministry of Health and Welfare consolidated operations with the Ministry of Labour to form the Ministry of Health, Labour and Welfare.[34] The Ministry of Transport and the Ministry of Construction, together with the National Land Agency and the Hokkaido Development Agency, formed the Ministry of Land, Infrastructure and Transport.[35] Before the merger the Ministry of Transport had 849 public corporations.[36]

The Ministry of Finance[37] retained autonomy, as did the Ministry of Agriculture, Forestry and Fisheries,[38] the Ministry of Justice[39] and the Ministry of Foreign Affairs.[40] The Ministry of International Trade and Industry took a new name, to become the Ministry of Economy, Trade and Industry (METI).[41] The Defence Agency was renamed the Ministry of Defence[42] and the Environmental Agency was renamed the Ministry of the Environment.[43]

Some of the agencies that were formerly within ministries have been detached. However, they are still operating under the jurisdiction of the ministries. As yet there is still no evidence that the restructuring of the ministries through the consolidation of duties will give the executive branch more power.

Restructuring the government system connotes changing the mind-set of the Japanese themselves, and this will take many years. Although the exposure to Western values and ideology since the mid-1800s has had an impact on Japanese lifestyles, the majority of Japanese people, who have never travelled beyond the country's borders, abide by a value system that has existed for hundreds of years. They belong to a rigid, hierarchical socio-political system that has been in place since the Meiji period, a system containing elements that can be traced back over a thousand years to when the Japanese were ruled by an elite aristocracy. In the twenty-first century they are ruled by a bureaucracy, with the power being firmly in the hands of an elite class of official.

## The elite officials: a world apart

There are more than 100,000 bureaucrats working in the ministries' headquarters in Kasumigaseki,. 20,000 of them holding the rank of 'career officer', who have entered the ministries after passing the taxing High Level Public Officials Examination and going through a gruelling series of interviews. There are only 1,000 officers with law degrees and an even smaller number are in top management in the ministries.[44] These are the elite officials who are entrusted by the Japanese to plan economic and social policies. They also draft the laws. Traditionally, the officials who climb to the top positions in the ministries have graduated from Tokyo University with a degree in Law. There is now a growing concern among the Japanese that the Tokyo University clique (*todaibatsu*) in the ministries creates an insular mentality and that graduates from other universities are discriminated against in the struggle for promotion at the top of the bureaucratic pyramid.

Officers holding degrees other than law can also experience discrimination. Since the ministries draft the laws, officers with law degrees are thought to be better equipped than officers who graduated with degrees in science and engineering, even if they come from Tokyo University. Some of the officers opt to enter the ministries because their families do not have personal contacts in big business. Some would-be officers apply to the ministries because family members are also in the same ministry.

Around twenty-five career officers are considered for grooming for elite rank when they enter the ministries. Along with their fellow career officers, during the initial three to five years, elite career officers are rotated to various divisions and assessed on their abilities. By their fifth year, the elite officers, who are mainly from MITI, MOF and the Ministry of Foreign Affairs (MOFA), are sent to universities overseas to earn degrees in law, economics and business administration. The elite are given three opportunities to go abroad. They may be posted in embassies, consulates or branch offices of special corporations or chartered corporations. Who is chosen for promotion and postings overseas can often be related to internal politics and connections.

The young elite officials work very hard and very long hours on their climb to the top. Even though they are in the upper echelons in the ministries, elite officers may live in drab, cramped, government-owned apartments early in their careers if they cannot afford separate housing. They receive no overtime payments and they must adhere to ministerial etiquette, obeying their superiors without question. Secretarial assistance is random, and many must do their own administration until they reach a relatively high rank. At the beginning of their careers, officers from the same class are promoted at the same time. However, through a gradual elimination process, only a few members will succeed in climbing to the upper echelons of their ministries.

The promotion of the rank-and-file is based on the seniority system in keeping with the ministries' hierarchical system. The seniority system makes advancement tediously slow. The senior members are retired (*katataki*, or 'tap on the shoulder') to make way for junior officials. As managerial positions become scarcer at the top, many officials opt to retire and move on to public corporations. An officer who is not promoted may retire if a fellow officer who entered in the same year receives a promotion.

Non-career officers are the second tier of officers in the ministries. They enter through a less demanding examination and act as support staff for career officers. Generally, they are not eligible for promotion to any higher position than middle management, nor do they generally have the same opportunities as career officers for rewards such as *amakudari*, although in recent years the number of post-retirement positions for non-career officers has increased. Non-career officers who have good connections in the ministries, such as family ties, may be sent on overseas duty as support staff for career officers, and they may be able to gain post-retirement positions in public corporations that are foundations or associations.

The Japanese call the world of the elite civil servant 'bureaucrat heaven' because, on retirement from government, they parachute into upper management positions in special corporations or other public corporations before moving on to private industry. A big incentive to become career bureaucrats is the second career after retirement at around fifty-five, ten years earlier than corporate executives, plus the double income, the easier schedule, and the release from the politics of Kasumigaseki.

The major reshuffling of the ministries has amounted to little more than putting one part of a ministry into another ministry,[45] with the basic structure of government remaining the same. Yamamura predicted in 1997 that the ministries would maintain a firm grip on the regulation of industry and that, despite domestic and foreign pressures to deregulate the market the ministries would continue to plan protectionist policies.[46]

The Cabinet has passed Koizumi's proposals for the privatization of special corporations, but the Diet has not been as co-operative. Since the number of special corporations has remained stable, and since bureaucrats administrate the reforms, it can be concluded that the bureaucracy will remain the dominant power in the 'ruling triad'.

# 5

## The Interpersonal Networks between Government and Business

### *Kone*: it's the connections that count

Personal connections (*kone*) play a vital role in Japanese daily life and are key ingredients in the glue that binds the ruling triad together. The right connections can facilitate an introduction to a reputable physician or entry into a good corporation, because without a personal recommendation it can be very difficult to get an interview. The Japanese have few natural resources and must rely on other countries for imports, a dependency that makes the government feel that the country is vulnerable. On the other hand, their personal networks and connections are resources they can depend upon, and of which they are very protective.

Connections between business and government can be created through marriage. The introduction of elite bureaucrats to the daughters of wealthy businessmen is often made through professional marriage brokers. There are marriages between budding bureaucrats and the daughters of high-ranking officials who serve in the grooms' ministries. Politicians in the LDP will marry the daughters of elder politicians to strengthen their position in their party. Former Prime Minister Takeshita's relationship with the construction industry was enhanced by the marriage of his daughter to the president of Kanemaru. These marriages tie families together, and the friends of the families form so-called 'marriage cliques' (*keibatsu*).

The bond between the bureaucracy, big business and politicians is fashioned from elaborate networks of formal and informal relationships between the three bodies, and generates an ideal environment for ministerial control over Japan's political economy. Sociologists have characterized it as: 'mutually dependent, obligatory, trusting, reinforcing parts of a whole'.[1] The relationship is often derived from the exchange of favours both large and small. It also is established among member of the same cliques *(batsu)* such as being alumni of the same university *(gakubatsu)*. Graduates from Tokyo University are members of a very influential clique in the ministries. This network plays a far more important role in Japanese society than does the 'old boys' network in the West.[2]

However, there is another side to this relationship. There is palpable concern among business owners that they may antagonize the administrators if they do not follow the prescribed guidance, and that they will suffer retribution in some form. There is also apprehension among business owners, who have affiliations with industrial associations, federations and public corporations, that if they do not comply with the objectives of the majority they will antagonize the other members. Therefore, although one of the elements in the relationship among the members of the 'ruling triad' may be mutual obligation, it must also be emphasized that there may be an underlying mistrust and a prevailing fear of alienation.

A consequence of the connections between business and the ministries can be seen in the use of the policy instrument 'administrative guidance' *(gyoseishido)* that is indicative in the Japanese system. All ministries have used the tool consistently, but MITI in particular has used this tool effectively since the 1950s to rationalize production and protect markets. In general, the objective of an industrial policy is to protect and nurture industries deemed to be vital to national interests. It can be said that the planning of industrial policies reflects the historical and cultural traditions of nations.[3] Furthermore, the methods used to implement policies are influenced by elements found in the socio-political systems.

In Japan, the regulation of industry can be directed through 'administrative guidance', a policy instrument used *ad hoc* and at the discretion of the ministries. There are no laws that limit the number of times the tool can be used, giving the ministries uncommon powers to regulate. Companies will usually receive notification requesting that they follow ministerial regulation. The directives are transmitted either in writing or by telephone, although a law in 1997 officially curtailed the use of the telephone. Companies rarely reject guidance, for a number of reasons. A primary factor that promotes the acquiescence to elite authority is the fear of future retribution in such forms as fines, and the rejection of permits and applications for patents and subsidies. There is also the concern of businessmen who are members of industrial associations that if they alone refuse to join the ranks of fellow members of the industrial associations, who wish to comply with the directives, they may face a boycott of their goods by those members.[4]

MITI began using 'administrative guidance' formally in 1952 in order to form cartels of industries designated as important to national interests, such as heavy industries and petrochemicals, protecting them from foreign competition. The Anti-monopoly Law was passed in 1947 but it was later reversed to allow the formation of cartels. After the oil shock of December 1973, MITI, in order to deal with problems developing from structurally damaged intensive-energy industries such as steel, petrochemicals and aluminum and the ensuing four-year recession, continued to use 'administrative guidance' to form anti-recession cartels. Kozo Yamamura, a professor of economics at the University of Washington, maintained that this policy was a continuation of policy implemented during the period of rapid economic growth and that 'the policies of coordinating investment and reducing risk of investment through cartels had become counterproductive'.[5,6]

In his article 'Success that Soured: Administrative Guidance and Cartels in Japan' (1982), to illustrate how 'administrative guidance' can be transmitted, and how the network of former bureaucrats in business and their former colleagues in the ministries facilitate the implementation of regulations, Yamamura quoted a report from the 8 January 1981 issue of *Nihon Keizai Shimbun*. This recounted the proceedings of a meeting between MITI officials and the directors of steel companies. The presidents and directors of steel companies and MITI officials would meet regularly at the Iron–Steel Building in Tokyo. The meeting was known as the Monday Club or 'General Session of the Market Policies Committee' (a cartel club)[7] that had been organized between MITI officials and industry in the early 1950s.

During the meeting, the director of the Iron and Steel Section of Basic Industries presented his case formally for a regulation to the directors of the steel companies. According to the newspaper article, the senior directors were former high-ranking MITI officials, thus implying that the meeting was merely a formality and that MITI's guidance would be accepted without question.

The increase of former MITI officials in the steel industry between 1983 and 1988 may indicate that MITI used 'administrative guidance' to implement the formation of cartels among steel manufacturers under the Structurally Depressed Industry Law.[8] Apparently, MITI's policy for the steel industry in the 1990s was the continued formation of cartels, and businesses that supplied steel companies wholeheartedly supported the policy wholeheartedly, because they were afraid that the industry would fail without regulation.[9]

Richard Katz, the senior editor of the *Oriental Economist Report*, claimed in 1998 that cartel-like policies were continuing to protect domestic markets even though the government insisted that many of the previous import barriers used, including tariffs, had been eliminated. He believed that members of industrial associations, such as petroleum, collude to fix prices while the Japan Fair Trade Commission turns a blind eye. Informal guidance may be given by ministries through their trade and industrial associations, whose members feel obliged to follow policy, such as purchasing solely from domestic producers. Katz claimed that companies fear retaliatory measures if they do not comply, pointing to Mitsubishi Heavy Industries as an example of a company that dared to purchase cheaper steel from a Korean firm at a third the cost of Japanese cartel-fixed prices. Mitsubishi was threatened with a cut-off of supplies and other penalties.[10]

'Administrative guidance' has given ministries the power to implement policy and this power is derived form the network of former ministry officials in business.

## Group unity/individual consent

The deference of the Japanese to elite ministry officials and acquiescence to group pressure facilitate the use of 'administrative guidance'. To the external observer, mutual trust and co-operation play a significant role in the interaction between individuals. This perception is an ideal. Realistically, the Japanese social system dictates that, in order to ensure a stable, secure and predictable environment, individual desires must remain subordinate to the needs of the group, and deviation from the set standards may result in harassment by other members or exclusion from the group. The fear of isolation pressures the individual to conform and this fear serves as a silent control mechanism over individuals who would behave in ways that are considered to be outside the norm.

Certainly during the 1990s as Japan's economy has deteriorated, banks and businesses have failed and unemployment figures risen, the Japanese citizens have come to understand that their environment is no longer as stable as they were led to believe. However, this state of affairs has not impinged upon the high degree of regimentation and, to date, has inspired mainly protests by opposition party members and journalists, whose roles fit into the category of 'protestors', and weak efforts at the grass roots level to resist central government policies.

The Japanese social system is a rigid hierarchy built up from group upon group but there is no single group that is directly on top of another. In other words, the structure of the system resembles a pyramid of horizontally positioned groups. First and foremost, the Japanese identify themselves as members of groups (for example, organizations such as corporations, government and educational institutions, divisions within those organizations and even home-towns). They do not identify themselves through their occupation or individual roles but through the institution where they work. Generally, when workers are questioned about their professions they will first refer to their employers ('I work for Mitsubishi Trading Company'). Chie Nakane, a well-known Japanese sociologist, maintains that even university degrees are not as important as the ranking of the institution where the individual received the degree.[11]

## Group pressures within organizations

Although Japanese people in their twenties and thirties may not feel as constricted as their parents were by the rigid social order, nevertheless they are still subject to the pressures to subordinate themselves to the demands of the group and to submit to higher authority in the workplace. The common perception among Westerners during Japan's economic expansion was that the Japanese corporate system was one of the major strengths of the country's political economy, that the system fostered loyalty among staff, and that the constant effort to integrate staff into the corporate culture secured a stable working environment. The lifetime employment system initiated after the war by big businesses to ensure a stable workforce promoted the image of a caring and nurturing employer whose fate was tied to that of the workers. The popular notion of Japanese corporate life is group unity and commitment to hard work to achieve corporate objectives. Employees participate in a daily exercise routine before starting work, management gives daily pep-talks to inspire commitment to the company, year-end bonuses are distributed to deserving staff, directors are personally involved in their staff's welfare, and superiors take their subordinates out drinking at the company's expense after working hours to encourage good communication and group harmony.

Observers now realize that this perception of the situation was superficial. Masafumi Matsuba, professor of economics at Ritsumeikan University, took a more pragmatic view, explaining that the most important factor supporting the integration of employees into large corporations was the high salaries and fringe benefits.[12] Another factor was 'military discipline and organization of human relations within the companies'.[13] When employees are asked if they enjoy the work environment they invariably reply, 'human relations are trying'(*ningen kankei*), illustrating the ongoing struggle to preserve group unity and harmony among staff.

A hierarchical corporate structure and the seniority system prevail in most of the institutions. Top management is usually composed of the oldest members of staff who have worked for their entire careers in the same organization.[14] Upper management will delegate daily operations to division managers. There can be as many as twenty members of staff per division, which is also structured as a hierarchy. The division managers delegate responsibilities to middle management, who will then delegate the work to division staff. Loyalty to the group leader is vital to the stability of the group. A worker rarely disagrees with his superior's decisions for fear of antagonizing him and falling out of favour. If an employee displeases his superior, the other members of the division may separate themselves from him and he then becomes isolated from the group. Since the Japanese identify themselves as members of groups and feel protected as such, isolation for them is an exceedingly unpleasant prospect. Any behaviour considered to be out of order, even mild dissent, may provoke isolation by other members of the division, who will move to protect their superior in the hope that he will regard them as loyal and reciprocate appropriately in the future. Despite the surface image of tranquillity there is a muted tension that workers learn to accept.

Group unity and loyalty to a higher authority are indicative of the Japanese social system. On the other hand, group unity tends towards a group insularity that prevents staff from sharing information with employees from different divisions. There is a fear of raising suspicion among the members of their own division if they share information that has no practical value with other divisions. Nowadays 'information-sharing' is a buzzword used by Japanese corporate executives who are trying to reform corporate operations, but group unity and the resulting insularity is inhibiting this freedom.

## What interpersonal networks can reap for local government

Karel van Wolferen was convinced that the network of interpersonal relationships between business and government served as a key support mechanism of the Japanese economy, and that there was no danger of it collapsing.[15] However, a network based on 'mutual obligation' can also construe a network of mutual protection, which prevented the early detection of the seriousness of Japan's economic condition. Nevertheless, having the right connections within the national ministries and the Diet is essential if local governments are to gain subsidies for local businesses and public works.

Ehime prefecture is a prime example of how large subsidies for public works were accessed by the governor, who had a solid interpersonal network in the national ministries. The prefecture generates about 36 per cent of local taxes, making it beholden to Tokyo for loans and subsidies for public works, education, health and welfare. Ehime does not have enough industry to support the issuance of bonds.[16] The term '30 per cent autonomy' is often used to refer to the fiscal control that central government's exercises over prefectures, thus pressuring them to abide by national policies.[17]

Ehime is the largest of four prefectures on the island of Shikoku, the smallest of the four major islands in the Japanese archipelago. The prefecture has an area of 5, 676.22 square kilometers with 162.5 kilometres of coastline, the fifth longest in Japan. The population at the time of writing is 1,489,732.[18] Matsuyama, the capital, has a

population of 450,000. Ehime is a rural area and its primary industries are agriculture, forestry and marine products. Its secondary
industries are mining, construction, paper and pulp production,
textiles, marine equipment, industrial machinery, electrical equipment and electrical components. There is also some shipbuilding and
petroleum refining.

Ehime ranks at 41 for personal income among the forty-eight
prefectures, 32 for personal income taxes, 25 in industrial output, 25
for agricultural produce and 30 for the size of its budget.[19] As one of
the less-well-endowed prefectures, Ehime is very dependent on the
largess from central government.

The former governor, Sadayuki Iga was an officer of the Ehime local
government and a staunch member of the LDP before he became
the governor, a position he held for twelve years until January 1999,
when he lost the election to Moriyuki Kato a retired official from
the Ministry of Education, who is a native of Ehime. During Iga's
incumbency, Ihei Ochi, Ehime's elected representative to the Lower
House in the national Diet, was the Minister of Construction (1987–8)
in Prime Minister Takeshita's first Cabinet. As a consequence, applications for public works projects were accepted in the first Takeshita
budget.[20]

Iga actively sought close relationships with the ministries and
frequently tapped into subsidies that brought profits for local firms
and provided his constituents with a convention centre, an international airport, a museum, a network of highways and tunnels
throughout Ehime's mountainous terrain, and the Kurushima Bridge
that links Ehime with Hiroshima on the main island of Honshu. The
bridge is under the management of the Honshu-Shikoku Bridge
Authority, the debt-ridden public corporation that Koizumi wanted
to merge with the Japan Highway Corporation.

The proof of Iga's close relationship with the officials in MITI,
MOC and the Ministry of Agriculture, Forestry and Fisheries (MAFA)
can be witnessed in the Foreign Access Zone (FAZ) installation in
the port city of Matsuyama. MITI initiated FAZ in 1993 to answer
the United States' demands that Japan open its markets to more
imports. In 1992 MITI wrote the Law on Extraordinary Measures
for the Promotion of Imports and the Facilitation of Foreign Direct
Investment in Japan, setting the stage for the construction of FAZ
installations throughout Japan. The first FAZ was built in Matsuyama.[21]

The FAZ was a co-operative effort between the three ministries and local businesses.

In April 1993 a company, comprising both government organizations and private corporations was established to manage FAZ.[22] The Ehime Foreign Access Zone Co. Ltd constructed a distribution centre for the handling of imported goods, and three exhibition halls (I.T.E.M. EHIME), one of which is the largest exhibition hall in the Shikoku-chugoku region.[23] The hall is suitable for many events with conference rooms, and projection and simultaneous translation equipment. The entire exhibition area covers 7,300 square meters.

The brochure released by the corporation claims that I.T.E.M. EHIME was built to 'promote local industries that serve Japan's increasingly international society'. Within I.T.E.M. EHIME is an Ehime Products and Tourism Centre divided into three areas where products from local industries are exhibited. There is I.T.E.M. World Mart for the display of imported foreign goods that are purported to have been introduced to Ehime consumers. Adjacent to the World Mart is a branch office of the Japan External Trade Organization (JETRO Support Centre), a special corporation under METI administration. The Centre promotes FAZ to foreign business owners when they visit, by providing information on doing business within the FAZ, market reports on foreign products that find consumer acceptance, and regional business reports.

A second FAZ installation is under construction. The Ehime Foreign Access Zone Co. states that the construction will 'involve building of a new port and roads connecting the facilities to the expressway system. The result will be a comprehensive upgrading of industrial infrastructure.' There are now twenty-two FAZ installations in designated port cities.[24]

In countries where economies are tightly regulated by central government, officials from local government cultivate close ties with central government officials to gain subsidies and loans. Regrettably, in Japan the money issued by both central government and local government for public works during the 1990s has not had the anticipated affect on the economy. On the contrary, it has resulted in the draining of both central and local government coffers.[25] Incredibly, much of the public works built in the 1990s, such as bridges, highways and convention centres, are not being utilized enough to have warranted their construction in the first place. The Japanese call them 'empty boxes' and there is growing opposition from local governments against the continuing commitment of the national ministries to the building dams and highways.[26]

Governor Iga also wanted to raise his prefecture's profile internationally by imitating the larger prefectures that had opened overseas representative offices in the 1980s and 1990s in order to promote local industries and to invite foreign investment. MITI urged small businesses to seek overseas markets aggressively, and easy loans from banks and FILP-funded banks such as the Japan Finance Corporation for Small Businesses encouraged them to ride on the tails of the big Japanese multinationals. Some of the prefectures could afford to operate offices independently, but budget constraints forced the majority to seek space in the offices of other Japanese organizations such as consulates, regional banks and JETRO, which has seventy-nine offices world-wide. Iga's contacts in MITI succeeded in gaining a place for his thirty-year-old son at the New York branch of JETRO. The son, an officer in his prefecture's government, was identified as a JETRO staff member during his year's tenure, but his duties primarily involved accompanying Ehime businessmen on tours around the United States. When he returned to Ehime he became the first director of a newly formed division for international business, attached to FAZ.[27] Other officers from Ehime prefecture government took over the son's seat at JETRO but their work was more specific to JETRO's needs than to Ehime's.[28]

Some Ehime residents cynically view the public works constructed during the last decade as Iga's attempt at self-glorification. For a rural area such as Ehime, where the size of its budget ranks 30th among the prefectures, industrial output ranks 25th and population is less than 1.5 million, it is difficult to determine how the government planned to use all the facilities over the long term. Ehime's trading partners are mainly in Asia, namely China and Korea, and export mainly agricultural commodities. As Japanese companies move production operations overseas for cheaper production, the industrialization of Ehime is highly uncertain.

Between 1997 and 2001 there were a total of eleven international trade fairs, but generally the halls of I.T.E.M. EHIME remain vacant. There is no noticeable change in the range of foreign imports in the World Mart. Foodstuffs, wines, toys, sporting equipment and other items on display overshadow industrial goods.

Traffic is relatively light on the new network of highways, and commuters to Hiroshima prefer riding the ferry than using the Kurushima Bridge because the toll is too expensive. The museum is a beautiful structure but there is not enough artwork to justify the construction.

Although Iga was expected to maintain control over Ehime politics, the recession prompted dissatisfied voters to replace him in January 1999. The reaction from local business to Governor Kato's election was favourable because, as a former ministry official, Kato had a good link to central government. However, Ehime, like the other prefectures, suffers from the burden of mounting debt, and the national debt is spiralling ever higher. Kato's connections in central government may not be as useful as the business owners had originally anticipated.

### Owners of small and medium-sized businesses: a link to the bureaucracy means a lot

It is believed in Japan that by hiring retired bureaucrats, private firms open an information pipeline to central government. Through their close ties to the ministries, former bureaucrats are able to gather information faster and more easily than anyone who is on the outside. Former bureaucrats can lobby on behalf of businesses to persuade the government from planning new rules and regulations that could affect production costs (for example, industrial safety standards) and put businesses at a disadvantage in the marketplace. Also, former bureaucrats can evaluate the type of guidance that businesses may receive (for example, cartels) and counsel accordingly.

Kent E. Calder, a professor of political science at Princeton University, theorized in 1989 that the owners of smaller businesses relied on former bureaucrats more than did the owners of larger businesses because they had less access to central government. A former bureaucrat on the board or in an upper management post of a smaller firm could 'equalize' the competition with the larger firms. He also proposed that firms located further from Tokyo relied more on former bureaucrats because they were more isolated from central government than companies closer to the capital, and therefore less capable of sustaining tight relationships with officials in ministries.[29]

Calder claimed that the overwhelming number of post-retirement positions was provided by public corporations. He also stated that

√ the network established between elite former bureaucrats in business and the bureaucracy can rigidify the system, thus preventing policy changes.

On the other hand, in his book entitled *Political Economic Study of Administraitve Guidance* (*Gyoseishido no Seiji Kiezai Gaku*), Kosuke Ooyama, a professor of Social Science at Tsukuba University,[30] questioned the validity of Calder's hypothesis that retired bureaucrats in smaller businesses were advantageous in accessing information, contending that there was no proof. He claimed that in MITI's case, the number of officers who took post-retirement positions in special corporations was high but that no statistics were provided by the Personnel Agency (1989) that revealed the number of officers who moved from special corporations to private corporations. He also contended that, compared to the other ministries, the number of MITI officers 'loaned' (*shukko*) to prefecture governments was not high but, that the number of officers 'loaned to other ministries as well as the number of employees from private companies 'loaned' to MITI was relatively high thus facilitating an information pipeline.[31]

The majority of owners of small businesses cannot afford to hire high-ranking officials,[32] but some may opt to hire lower-ranking officers or public servants who have worked for special corporations and chartered corporations. And having a former bureaucrat on board is by no means an insurance policy for small and medium-sized businesses. In the month of October 2001 alone, small and medium-sized business bankruptcies rose by 11.7 per cent, or 1,911 compared to October 2000.[33] The prospects for small businesses in 2003 look dismal as well. According to the results of a survey released by Osaka Shinkin Bank conducted among 1,200 small and medium-sized firms with accounts at the credit union, Osaka small businesses owners predict that they will fare no better than last year, which was as dreary as 2001. Among the reasons given were the fall in orders from client firms who were also performing poorly, and the increasing competition.[34]

It is a constant struggle for survival. Owners of small and medium-sized businesses must cultivate a strong network within the business community and government to keep up-to-date with the latest political and economic news, to maintain as stable and predictable an environment as possible for their firms.

The story of the CEO of a medium-sized chemical company (referred to as 'M Company')[35] provides a good example of the ways interpersonal networks and the right connections can help owners to expand operations, both domestically and internationally. Tokyo-based M Company was established in 1941 as a producer of special chemicals for the war effort. After the war, the founder continued operations, avoiding competition with large manufacturers by producing a small range of special chemicals. MCI administered the chemical industry during the war, and since M Company had produced for the war effort it retained a good relationship with MITI after the war. The founder's connections with ministry officials undoubtedly helped to secure subsidies. Between 1952 and 1977 the company received a number of subsidies from MITI for research and development. The founder's strategy included opening a niche in the domestic marketplace by producing new chemical products and expanding production overseas. Both strategies were ambitious, but the company has achieved both goals during the sixty-plus years it has been in business.

The founder's interpersonal network in government helped him to import new and inexpensive technologies in the 1950s and 1960s.[36] His connections in MITI may have expedited his application for patents, licences and permits. He hired an officer from the Japan Finance Corporation as Senior Managing Director and General Manager of Executive Affairs, thus placing the company in a more favourable position to receive long-term, low-interest loans.

When the founder died, his son succeeded him. M Company tied up with a major pharmaceutical firm and a clock manufacturer, supplying them with special chemicals. The CEO, looking ahead at foreign markets, opened up a sales office in Hong Kong in the early 1980s. Eyeing markets in Europe and the United States, M Company engaged in a joint venture with a major trading company, a wise move because the trading company had long-established distribution channels. The trading company did not manufacture the same kinds of chemicals thus the relationship was, and continues to be, mutually beneficial. M Company supplies technical information and production acumen, and the trading company supplies investment and distribution. The CEO took advantage of the relationship by hiring an employee from the trading company who was based in Europe for many years. He knew how to conduct business in

European countries and was an appropriate liaison with his former employer. Another pay-off was that the vice-chairman of the trading company had been an elite official in MITI, giving M Company additional connections with the ministry.

The CEO never takes his connections for granted, working tirelessly to maintain and extend his interpersonal network in business and government. He is the friend of a former prime minister who graduated from the same university (*gakubatsu*). He is the president of his district's Chamber of Commerce and Industry, a chartered corporation managed by MITI's Industrial Policy Bureau. It maintains branch offices throughout Japan and sixty offices around the world, some of them housed in JETRO offices. He also serves simultaneously in other small and medium-sized business organizations managed by MITI. Through participation he is in constant contact with the other owners of small and medium-sized businesses and with the elite officials who manage them.

Good management, wise corporate strategies, product diversification and expansion into overseas markets have been important reasons for M Company's survival during the recession. However, the CEO also needed a solid interpersonal network with central government officials and owners of big businesses in order to sustain long-term growth and stability.

Edward J. Lincoln believed that changing a few elements in the system would not promote reform because the Japanese system as a whole was 'interconnected', and estimated that 70 per cent of the population had vested interests. Lincoln identified the most significant reasons why the Japanese seem unable to move on reform: social conformity and their reluctance to part with their values.[37]

# 6

## The ties that Bind: *amakudari* and *shukko*

### Definition

The literal translation of the term *amakudari* is 'descent from heaven' and refers to the practice of bureaucrats taking post-retirement positions in public and private corporations. The retired officials receive full salaries from their new organizations along with their civil service pensions. *Amakudari* began in the 1930s when the government started to strictly regulate the economy for the war effort. Business owners employed bureaucrats in order to determine future government directives.

*Amakudari* was fostered by the civil service after the war because bureaucrats were retired by the age of fifty-six or fifty-seven, earlier than in the private sector, to make room in the ministries for younger officers. The ministries wanted to provide retiring officials with a new source of income that enhanced their pensions. Ostensibly the system provided an incentive for officers who would otherwise seek employment in the private sector rather than the civil service, where salaries were lower. However, the system also served the interests of the bureaucracy because it created a network of former bureaucrats and their erstwhile colleagues throughout the public and private sectors, thereby increasing the bureaucracy's power to control economic and industrial policies. In effect, *amakudari* has acted to establish a control mechanism in the political economic system, expediting the use of such policy instruments as 'administrative guidance', discussed in Chapter 5. The relationship between a bureaucrat and his former colleagues, who are posted in businesses in a sector under their ministry's administrative jurisdiction, automatically tightens the ministry's grip on that sector. Logically, the more territory there is within a ministry's jurisdiction, the more positions there may be in companies whose industries are within that jurisdiction. Originally, the elite bureaucrats were the main beneficiaries of *amakudari* but gradually officers in middle management *(kacho)* as well as non-career officers have also come to be included in the system.

### Rules and regulations

The National Personnel Agency places bureaucrats who have reached retirement into private and public corporations. The agency encourages business owners to hire bureaucrats in an advertisement that it runs on its website: 'Wouldn't you like to use the skills of civil servants?' The advertisement shows an executive sitting at a desk explaining a document to staff. The executive appears to be a retired official. The words beneath the picture read: 'His abilities are amazing! Wouldn't it be great if civil servants could come to work for our companies after they retire?'

The agency reassures companies that its 'use of the human resource system' is fair and impartial, and that it will take care of the details, instructing interested parties to apply through the Federation of Economic Organization *(keidanren)* whose members are in big business. The agency also promises that it will make inquiries at the ministries for employees who will meet the companies' needs.[1]

Ministry officials also find post-retirement positions for fellow colleagues in the industries their ministries administrate, but the National Public Service Law stipulates that bureaucrats cannot, for a period of two years, legally move directly to positions in private companies attached to the sectors their ministries regulate. However, they can move immediately to special corporations, public corporations and industrial associations, where they linger for two years on a salary before going on to the private sector.

### Manifestations of *amakudari*

The Japanese call their country 'bureaucrats' heaven' because of the lucrative post-retirement positions awaiting elite bureaucrats after they retire.[2] There are various ways the ministries can manipulate the *amakudari* system through the shrewd use of special corporations and public corporations, thus ensuring a secure future for their retirees:

(i)   if retired bureaucrats are on the staff of two organizations simultaneously (for example, advisers and board members) they can receive two salaries plus ministry benefits

(ii)  there are instances where bureaucrats are sent by their ministries to work in associations and public corporations while they are still engaged by their ministries (and drawing a salary). They then migrate to the private sector without waiting out the two-year period of grace

(iii) another option for bureaucrats is to remain attached in some way to special corporations through their subsidiaries or in other public corporations (as advisers or members of boards) while working for private businesses, and receiving salaries from both employers

(iv)  the period of stay in special corporations is usually limited to two years because positions are much sought after. However, there are instances when periods of stay can be as long as six years

(v)   positions in special corporations are given to elite officials who are too young to be retired but who are considered to be nearing the end of their careers. The 'gift' is actually a sign to officials that they will not be promoted much higher in their ministries, but that their labour and loyalty are appreciated. These officials return to their ministries to serve another two years before retiring, and some move on to public corporations and industrial associations. The high salaries that top management receives make special corporations particularly enticing to officials, who jostle for the positions. However, they may remain longer in public corporations, especially if they cannot find employment in the private sector.

## A variation on the *amakudari* theme: *shukko*

The term *shukko* means 'on loan to another company'. In the bureaucracy it signifies the temporary posting of ministry officials for periods of one to three years of duty in the prefecture government offices, in special corporations and in other types of public corporation. Although the officials are still connected to their ministries they are identified as officers of the organizations where they have been transferred temporarily. *Shukko* posts are considered to be temporary but can develop into permanent positions in public corporations and prefecture government offices. In essence, *shukko* can be the catalyst for *amakudari*.

### *Amakudari* to special corporations and public corporations

Special corporations and public corporations can facilitate the smooth migration of retiring bureaucrats to upper management positions in private firms. The process is called 'side-slipping' or *yokosuberi*. According to an official government report released on 26 December 2002, altogether 1,273 bureaucrats took post-retirement positions in public and private corporations that year. The number of bureaucrats, including non-career officers, who 'side slipped' to public corporations, was 461 (42 per cent), and the number of officials who took positions in special corporations was 67 (5 per cent). The report stated that the former administrative vice-minister of the Ministry of Land, Infrastructure and Transport moved on to an independently administered institution (IAI) that promotes proper real estate transactions. The ministry's personnel division revealed that a third of retiring officials, or 103, took positions in public corporations that are foundations (*zaidan*), a number it contends is not high if compared to the other ministries.

The same government report also pointed to the migration of various elite ministry officials, among them, the administrative vice-minister from the Ministry of Public Management, Home Affairs, Posts and Telecommunications who took the position of president of the National Governors Association. The administrative vice-minister from the former Ministry of Labour migrated to the Labour Welfare Corporation, a special corporation.[3]

There is the possibility that the official report may not be a reliable source. According to the *Asahi Shimbun* in its 28 March 2002 issue, the official reports from the Personnel Agency may divulge as little as 5 per cent of the number of elite bureaucrats who take post-retirement positions in both public and private organizations. Regardless of the number, Japanese people generally view special corporations and public corporations as 'saucers' (*ukezara*) for retiring bureaucrats.

Before the ministries merged in 2001, each ministry managed a certain number of special corporations. When some of the ministries merged their special corporations were put under one roof. For example, when the Ministry of Construction merged with the Ministry of Transportation, the National Land Agency and the Hokkaido Development Agency it brought along its corporations, as did the other agencies. Among the corporations the MOC brought in were the Japan Highway Corporation, the Government Housing Loan Corporation, the Metropolitan Expressway Corporation, the Honshu–Shikoku Bridge Authority, the Urban Development Corporation and the Japan Regional Development Corporation, a corporation that was managed jointly by MITI and the National Land Agency. The corporation is still managed by both the newly formed ministry and METI. The Ministry of Transportation's special corporations included the New Tokyo International Airport Authority, Kansai International Airport Company Ltd, and the Shikoku Railway Company.

The ministries that did not merge retained their special corporations. The Ministry of Foreign Affairs has two corporations, and the Ministry of Agriculture, Forestry and Fisheries has seven. The two economic ministries, METI and MOF, retained their special corporations, MOF with four and METI with twelve, which, as was mentioned above, includes the Japan Regional Development Corporation. METI also joins with the Ministry of Education, Culture, Sports, Science and Technology to manage the Japan Nuclear Cycle Development Institute.

Compared to METI, MOF may appear to be 'special corporation poor', but MOF officials need not worry about finding positions in special corporations or in any public corporation. Johnson reported that a disgruntled former official of the Ministry of Agriculture accused MOF of increasing the budgets of the ministries that opened their public corporations to MOF retirees.[4] The former bureaucrat's accusations could be correct. Tsutomu Kuji a political and environmental activist who has written about scandals involving the Ministry of Construction and the Ministry of Health and Welfare, and industries in their respective jurisdictions, published a book in 1998 about the *amakudari* practices of MOF officials. In *The Bureaucrat's Kingdom: Japan's Downfall* (*Kanryo Kokka Nippon no Botsuraku*) he indicated that, traditionally

MOF officials served regularly as vice-presidents or directors of special corporations that were managed by the other ministries. They go to such METI special corporations as the New Energy Development Corporation (NEDO), the Japan Finance Corporation, the Metal Mining Corporation, and the Japan National Oil Corporation.[5] MOF elite gain positions in the Government Housing Loan Corporation that is managed by MOC. MOF officials regularly side-slip to positions of vice-president of the Agriculture, Forestry and Fisheries Finance Corporation, managed by the Ministry of Agriculture, Forestry and Fisheries.[6] On the other hand, MOF ordinarily will not open the doors of its public corporations to officials of the other ministries. Although it allows METI officials to enter the Development Bank of Japan,[7] its other three corporations, the National Finance Corporation, the Japan Bank for International Co-operation and Japan Tobacco Incorporated, are for MOF officials only. The prize position for a MOF official is the presidency of the Development Bank of Japan, which usually goes to the administrative vice-minister. With MOF's 900 public corporations[8] and government-related financial institutions, MOF officials have many options for 'side-slipping'.

Kuji wrote that, in 1997, the prime minister's office announced in a 'White Paper on Public Corporations' that 7,080 bureaucrats had moved to 26,089 public corporations and that 184 retired MOF officials received top management posts in 87 public corporations connected to MOF.[9] He maintained that even though the organizations had different names their responsibilities were remarkably similar and it was obvious that they were places for *amakudari*. Among the thirteen examples he provided were the Financial Economic Research Centre (*Kinyu Keizai Kenkyujo*), Financial Research Institute (*Zaisei Kinyu Kenkyujo*) and the Research Committee for Financial Situations (*Kinyu Zaisei Jijo Kenkyukai*).

METI, the other economic ministry, manages twelve special corporations. In terms of the number of *yokosuberi* positions available to its elite officials, the Japan External Trade Organization (JETRO) offers the most with its seventy-nine offices world-wide. The most popular of the overseas offices are the ones in New York (referred to as the 'golden apple'), London and Paris. Positions in the overseas offices of the Japan National Oil Corporation (JNOC)[10] are also popular with offices in London, Paris, Moscow, Beijing, Jakarta, Sydney, Abu Dhabi, Washington, DC, and Houston.

There is an intense competition among the elite for positions in the JNOC. Kuni Komatsu handed in his resignation in 1998 after admitting that the corporation had a mountain of bad debt, but the vice-president, the director and the director of finance, who were ex-MOF officials, remained. Komatsu[11] had served almost six years as president, a position that is traditionally reserved for retired METI administrative vice-ministers. Although he had climbed to the position of vice-minister he had no experience in energy administration. The Minister of Commerce and Industry insisted that Komatsu's successor should be an economist with experience in energy administration otherwise it would be impossible to restructure the corporation. According to the 11 June 1998 edition of *Sankei Shimbun*, when Komatsu was moving to take a second term, it was rumoured that Yuji Tanahashi,[12] a former administrative vice-minister (retired in 1991) would succeed Komatsu because he had enough power to push Komatsu out; however, Komatsu continued to serve. Other names of former METI officials said to be candidates for president of the JNOC were Noboru Hatakeyama, former chairman of JETRO, and Kichio Sakamoto, at the time of writing, an adviser at Mitsubishi Bank.

The harsh criticism levelled at the JNOC for withholding vital information regarding the extent of outstanding loans as well as complaints about JNOC officials moving to oil companies that had relations with the JNOC, should have forced the appointment of a professional administrator from outside METI, but tradition prevailed and METI officials continue to serve as president. Former METI official Yoshiro Kamata is the current president.

The vice-minister of the Ministry of Construction usually lands the top position of president of the Japan Highway Corporation. He may then move on to the position of president of the Association for the Establishment of Highways, a public corporation that was described in Chapter 2. The majority of staff have moved from the MOC, from the former National Land Agency and from the Japan Highway Corporation, an illustration of massive *amakudari*.[13]

### *Amakudari* to the private sector

A big incentive drawing the Japanese to careers in the national ministries are the positions in upper management in private corporations and the comfortable salary that they receive simultaneously with their pensions from the ministries. The two years of service, or *yokosuberi*, in a special corporation is beneficial to officials because they can make connections to future employers if they have not already done so during their time in the ministries. Komatsu's resignation inflamed political opposition against *amakudari* and the JNOC was condemned because the officers in top management moved to petroleum companies and other large corporations with whom they made contact while at the JNOC. In his book Kazuma Tsutsumi charts in detail the routes of former elite METI officials after they had exited the JNOC, indicating that they became presidents of oil companies such as Indonesia Oil, and other large corporations such as the Japan Steel Pipe Co.[14] The JNOC top management also find positions as advisers in Japanese subsidiaries and affiliates of multinational companies such as Mobile and Shell.

According to Tsutsumi, after Tamotsu Katsutani served as the president, he moved on to the position of adviser at Indonesian Oil, gradually climbing to become vice-president and finally to chairman of the board. He served simultaneously as the president of the Oil Mining Federation and the chairman of Northern Oil.

Yuhiko Matsuo was president of the JNOC in 1989 before moving on to Indonesia Oil where he served as an advisor and later as president. In 1991, Koji Fukuzawa became the director-general at the JNOC and then moved on to the Japan Steel Pipe Co.

Tsutsumi charted the paths of METI officials after they left JETRO. Toru Toyoshima was an interesting case of a former METI official who side-slipped 'backwards'. After leaving the Export-Import Bank of Japan in 1984 he assumed the position of vice-president at Cosmo Oil. Then he went to Abudabi Oil as president. He then did an about face and became the chairman of JETRO. At the time of writing, he is the Chairman of the Japan Economic Foundation (FEF), an organization linked with JETRO.

Isao Kubogawa was posted to JETRO Bangkok in 1990. After leaving the special corporation he assumed the position of managing director of Tobu Department Stores. METI's territory covers the retail industry.

MOF officials tend to migrate to top management in financial institutions, security firms, life insurance companies and any business that may be connected to MOF's sectors. The Central Bank of Japan is the highest position a MOF elite official can receive. Retired MOC officials will most often find post-retirement posts in construction-related corporations. Tsutsumi contends that the Ministry of Public Management, Posts and Telecommunications will be the most powerful ministry in the twenty-first century because it administrates the telecommunications industry. The companies in which retired officials find positions are engaged in communication systems and satellites. There are also NTT East and NTT West which remain special corporations managed by the ministry.[15]

### *Amakudari* to research institutes

Kuji contends that, since the current sentiment is critical of special corporations, MOF officials are using universities and research institutes to wait out the two-year period of grace. According to the *Mainichi Shimbun*, retired METI administrative vice-ministers move to the Industrial Research Institute, a foundation that was established in 1976. Purportedly the institute promotes 'research and understanding.'[16]

Two of METI's special corporations have funded the institute: the Japan Corporation for the Promotion of Bicycle Racing and the Japan Auto Racing Association. Yuji Tanahashi retired in 1991 and entered the institute in 1993.[17] The *Mainichi Shimbun* contended that administrative vice-ministers regularly took positions in the institute, but Seiji Yamazaki, the director, maintained that this was coincidental. The *Mainichi Shimbun* alleged that Tanahashi used the secretarial staff for private business without reimbursing the institute, but Yamazaki also maintained that Tanahashi's business was related to research. Hideaki Kumano[18] migrated to the institute after he resigned from METI in 1994.

### *Amakudari* to political office

A major reason why the ministries have been able to implement policies with relative ease is the continuous support from the National Diet that has been dominated by the LDP for most of the post-war period in Japan. With the exception of Kyoto prefecture, which had a Communist administration for thirty years, the LDP has also dominated politics in the prefectures. Elite bureaucrats retire from the ministries to run for political office, usually on the LDP ticket. Is has been estimated that 21 per cent of the seats in the House of Representatives were held by former bureaucrats between 1955 and 1984.[19] Hiroshi Kumagai, who is mentioned in Chapter 4, left MITI to run for a seat in the House of Councillors on the LDP ticket. The tie-up between former ministry officials in the Diet and their previous colleagues intensifies the relationship between the LDP and the ministries who regulate the traditional support groups connected with small business, telecommunications, agriculture, construction and transportation companies.

As of July 1994, there were twenty-six former bureaucrats serving as governors of prefectures, and all of them were members of the LDP. Seventeen had migrated from the Ministry of Home Affairs.[20] Ichiro Murakawa, a political scientist who has written extensively about the Japanese Constitution, did an interesting study on elite officials in his book *Japan's Bureaucrats* (*Nihon no Kanryo*). He found that elite officials serve as both governors and vice-governors of the larger prefectures. Officials in middle management (the *kacho* class) will serve as vice-governors in the medium-sized prefectures regardless of whether they have influence in their ministries. The officers often serve as the directors of general affairs in the governors' offices.[21]

## *Shukko* to local government: an extension of ministerial control

Ministries 'loan' staff to the prefectural governments for periods of up to three years, justifying the postings by pointing out that the officers serve as a pipeline between central and local government, where they study the region and relay information about the local government to Tokyo. The opponents of this type of 'loan' system argue that the transferring of ministry officials to local government proves unequivocally that the national government does not trust local government administrators.[22] The officials posted in the prefectures can be watchdogs for their ministries (*haku tsuke* or 'placing a hawk') and, consequently, can become the instruments for controlling policies at government level.

Japanese children learn in school that local government relies on central government, and that local government officials administrate the work of central government.[23] The Council on Local Authorities for International Affairs (CLAIR) represents Japanese local government overseas. The organization, managed by the Ministry of Public Management, Home Affairs, Posts and Telecommunications, releases the annual publication *Local Government in Japan*, which explains the structure of local government and its relationship to central government: Chapter 1, Section 8 states:

> The philosophy underlying the Local Autonomy Act is that the interferences by central government should be kept to a minimum and should consist of advice, recommendations and technical support. In reality, the central government's involvement in local government affairs is extensive. However, the process is not wholly one-way. Just as local authorities seek approval and subsidies from various government agencies, those same ministries and agencies need information from local authority.[24]

Ministry officials are posted in the local government offices not only in capital cities but throughout the prefectures as well. In 1993, the *Mainichi Shimbun* conducted a survey of ministry officials on 'loan' to local government. As of December 1993, 770 officials with a rank higher than the *kacho* class (middle management) were posted in local government offices.[25] Ishikawa Prefecture is known as the Kasumigaseki of the North because it has a concentration of ministry officials in its government offices: in 1993, there were twenty.

The same survey asked local government officers for their opinions regarding the positive and negative aspects of having ministry officials in their offices. The officers from Ishikawa prefecture answered that the merits of having the officials were that they were members of the central ministry 'clan' (*jinpa*) and, therefore, a good pipeline to Tokyo. Also, they were a valuable resource in offices that were under-staffed. The negative side of having ministry officials around was that the ministries presumed that their officials should be planning local policy, and that too many of them tended to stultify local government.[26]

Officers of the *kacho* class in the Yamanashi prefecture government answered that, while some of the officials for the ministries were very skilled, others did not make the grade. They felt that the number of ministry officials should be reduced because there were excellent local government officers whose administrative skills should be nurtured.

By pointing to Tokyo metropolitan government, where there were thirty-six officers on loan from the ministries, *Mainichi Shimbun* illustrated the control that the ministries exercise over local government. Koku Narita, a *kacho* in Human Resources, told the newspaper that the loan of ministry officials to local government was like 'borrowing a sun visor' (*hisashi kashi*). Local government requests favours (for example, subsidies) from central government and should therefore reciprocate by co-operating with central government.

*Mainichi Shimbun* sent out another questionnaire concerning *shukko* at the end of 1993, to 100 officers ranked above the *kacho* class in the central ministries and other government agencies and to politicians in both the House of Representatives and House of Councillors. Taking into consideration that there was a strong political movement to reform the bureaucracy, the answers were surprising and, indeed, indicated that the political environment was still steeped in conservatism. Although 33 per cent of members in the House of Councillors were opposed to the system, they were heavily outnumbered by the 41 per cent of the members who answered that 'loaning' was necessary to provide a pipeline between local and central government. Ironically, only 5 per cent believed that ministry officials were skilful administrators. Members of *Komeito*, the New Japan Party and the Pioneer Parties were also in favour of *shukko*.

Conversely, the Communist Party was totally opposed to the system, as were 57 per cent of the members of the Socialist Party. Opinions expressed about *shukko* by the opposition were: (i) there should be a law that regulates the number of officers loaned to the prefectures; (ii) local government should try to think in terms of self-governing; and (iii) local government must cultivate its own elite class of officers.

Murakawa argued that although members of the National Diet talked about the importance of devolution, the loan of ministry officials to prefecture governments effectively stopped the process.[27]

Despite the conservatism in the Diet, another national public survey conducted by *Mainichi Shimbun* in 1993 revealed a more liberal attitude among voters – 41 per cent were opposed to *shukko* while 40 per cent were in favour of the system when deemed necessary. Only 3 per cent of those polled were completely in favour of *shukko*.

The ministries send officials to the branch offices of their special corporations. These officials can also monitor and advise on local government policies and serve effectively to extend the ministries' networks throughout Japan. The Japan Highway Corporation, the Japan Finance Corporation for Small Businesses, JETRO and the Japan Regional Development Corporation are among the special corporations with numerous branch offices.

### *Shukko* to other government agencies can function as *yokosuberi*

Older elite officials nearing the end of their careers may be loaned to other agencies for temporary duty, but there are instances where these positions can lead to better ones in private industry. Tsutsumi gave an example of Hiromichi Eguchi, a MITI officer, who in 1977 was loaned to the Defence Agency where he served as director of the Equipment-procurement Bureau where traditionally MITI officers are sent for duty. Instead of returning to MITI he moved to the Japan National Oil Corporation and later assumed the position of president of Arabian Oil. Eventually he became chairman and then a consultant for the company, and while he was consulting for Arabian Oil he took the position of managing director of the Japan Association of Defence Industries.

Tsutsumi claimed that companies employing MITI officials, who had been loaned to the Defence Agency, developed close ties to the agency. Some of Eguchi's successors in the Defence Agency's Equipment-procurement Bureau followed similar paths. Their routes took them to top positions in Sony Corporation, Sharpe Corporation, Tokyo Marine Insurance Company, Nihon Soken, and Sumitomo Electric.[28]

### *Shukko* to public universities

The Ministry of Education, Culture, Sports, Science and Technology administrates Japan's national, prefectural and city universities, and loans officials to these institutions. Many of the professors are public servants (*komuin*) and must follow strict regulations. For example, unlike professors in the United States and the United Kingdom, they cannot own or invest in businesses. The ministry provides the funding for research conducted abroad. At times ministry officials will accompany professors abroad when they speak at conferences. Since both public and private universities receive subsidies from the government they are obliged to invite ministry officials to lecture, the terms ranging from one to five years. Retired officials may be offered positions in universities. An example of this type of *amakudari* is former president of the Japan National Oil Corporation, Koji Matsumoto,[29] who was an official in MITI before he was appointed Counsellor in the Japanese Embassy in Canberra, Australia. In 1990 he moved to the JNOC as general director of the General Administration Department. In 1993 he became a professor in the Graduate School of Policy Science, Saitama University.

## Round and round it goes

Special corporations and public corporations act as the facilitators of the *amakudari* system, a system that establishes an organic interdependence between the bureaucracy, businesses, and national and local political organizations. This interdependence rigidifies the Japanese political economic system and defies reform because it is self-perpetuating.

On 13 November 2000, Iwanami Booklet No. 425 carried an interview with Tsutsumi conducted by Jiro Yamaguchi. The interview was entitled 'White Paper on *Amakudari* in the Bureaucracy' (*Kanryo Amakudari Hakusho*). Tsutsumi presented a proposal for the elimination of *amakudari*, which he named 'a hotbed of corruption'. His proposal called for setting a fixed age for retirement in the civil service and eliminating early retirement entirely. Tsutsumi wanted to stop *amakudari* to profit-making enterprises and to dissolve all special corporations, public corporations and industrial associations. In addition, no longer would elite officials be permitted to side-slip to special corporations and public corporations and they would have to wait for three to five years before running for political office. Tsutsumi emphasized that the career paths of bureaucrats should be equalized and that there should no longer be a discrepancy between the ranks of career and non-career offices.

When he was asked if *amakudari* would decrease, Tsutsumi responded that the numbers of retired officials moving to private businesses would increase despite State Minister Ishihara's insistence that all *amakudari* resulting from pressures from the ministries would be eliminated, that all relevant information would be made public, and that there was an aim to reach a fundamental solution to the problem. Tsutsumi claimed that the government makes public only 5 per cent of the actual figures.

# 7
# The Japan External Trade Organization: The Scent of a Ministry

JETRO is a case of a special corporation that was established originally to function as a promoter of Japanese small business exports but which has come to function as a vehicle that increases the territory, and consequently, the power, of the establishing ministry.

Opponents of special corporations contend that, while the corporations were established on the principle that their work promoted the interests of the nation, they have come to serve the interests of the ministries and should be dissolved or privatized, for the following reasons: (i) the ministries use their corporations as temporary landing spots for retired elite officials until they can legally move on to positions in the private sector. The consequential interpersonal relationships between retired bureaucrats in business and their ministries intensifies the ministries' administrative control over the economy; (ii) by posting ministry officials at the branches of special corporations in the prefectures, the ministries effectively extend their controls over local government policies; and (iii) special corporations breed subsidiaries that also provide post-retirement positions for retired bureaucrats.

These criticisms reflect the concern of Japanese citizens that the control mechanisms used by the bureaucracy over the political economy also inhibit the reform of the economy, which has been in continual crisis since 1990. Critics argue that basic to economic reform is the dissolution of institutions, among them special corporations, that serve to perpetuate bureaucratic power and a rigid and archaic governing system.

The reform of special corporations began in 1995. Since then the government has been tackling the problem of defining exactly what these corporations do, and how they receive and spend funds. Audits of special corporations' accounts that were conducted by the government in 1997 revealed that, while some of them carried enormous outstanding loans, they were continuing to operate – for example, the Japan Highway Corporation and the Japan National Oil Corporation.

Koizumi plans to dissolve all special corporations and chartered corporations by either merging them and then privatizing the merged entities, thus dissolving them altogether, or converting thirty-eight of them into independent administrative institutions (IAI).[1] The government will review the work of IAIs to ascertain whether they are managed efficiently, and whether their work is in the national interest.

Cabinet State Minister of Administrative and Regulatory Nobuteru Ishihara told reporters at a press conference on 22 November 2002 that he hoped that Diet members would share the understanding that the continuation of special corporations was a problem. He gave the Japan External Trade Organization (JETRO) as an example, stating that both he and the Minister of Economy, Trade and Industry were amazed to learn that the corporation issued a pamphlet advertising import promotion. Their reaction inferred that these duties had become extraneous because of Japan's continuing recession and contracting domestic demand. Also, Ishihara was insinuating that some corporations were no longer serving the function they were originally established to serve and that they were contriving work in order to justify their budgets and continue operating.

It was not the first time that JETRO's activities as an import promoter had been questioned. In 1995, Murayama's programme for the reform of special corporations focused media attention on special corporations. The Opinion Page of *News Asahi* (Internet *Asahi Shimbun*) ran an article on 9 January 1995 about Murayama's struggle to convince the ministries to consolidate some of the smaller special corporations. It reported that the now defunct Pioneer Party had called for the dissolution of the Price Stabilization of Silk Yarn and Sugar Corporation and the Promotion of Agriculture and Livestock Corporation, both under the administration of the Ministry of Agriculture, Forestry and Fisheries. The ministry balked, claiming that the corporations would continue to protect consumers by planning strategies that would stabilize prices. However, the ministry did consider merging the two corporations. In 1999, the two entities were united under the name the Agriculture and Livestock Industries Corporation (ALIC).[2]

The *Asahi* article noted that when the Murayama Administration conducted hearings on the restructuring of special corporations, MITI was reluctant to participate and wanted to know if the restructuring concerned the number of corporations or if it was related to financing. The article claimed that the ministries were changing the objectives of their corporations by contriving new roles. The paper called this 'skill at disguising' (*henshin no gijutsu*) pointing to JETRO as an example of a special corporation that had been established in 1956 for the purpose of promoting Japanese exports: 'Now when you phone the JETRO headquarters the receptionist answers: "JETRO, import promoter".'

On 13 June 1995 the front page of *Sankei Shimbun* published an article by its Washington, DC, correspondent Yoshihisa Komori titled 'Is JETRO Running Wild?' (*'JETERO Boso!?'*). Next to the story was a photograph of JETRO's Tokyo headquarters. Komori pointed his finger to the editorial by JETRO New York president, Nobuya Noguchi in the April edition of *Inside/Outside Japan*. The monthly newsletter, published by JETRO New York, was sent unsolicited to opinion leaders in business, government and academia. In his editorial, Noguchi wrote very positively about former United States Secretary of Defense Robert McNamara's book *In Retrospect: The Tragedy of Lessons of Vietnam*. He wrote in part:

> Finally, on this 20th anniversary of the end of the war, he [McNamara] has made public his close examination of how he and other policy makers were gradually pulled into a dubious war. It is in this process that he repeatedly admits his mistakes. This is a courageous act. I cannot recall a single instance from among Japanese policy makers who, following Japan's defeat, did anything remotely similar.

According to Komori, one reader, William Triplet ii, had taken exception to Noguchi's reference to the Vietnam War as 'dubious'. Triplet, an aide to Republican Senator Robert Bennet, who was a member of the Senate Committee of Foreign Relations and a recipient of the newsletter, protested that Noguchi was the president of an organization which was established to promote foreign trade and economic co-operation and therefore should not be involved in commenting on political issues.

Komori claimed that there was opposition in the National Diet to the continuation of JETRO because (i) it no longer served its original function as a trade promotion organization; (ii) JETRO was an underground MITI (*kakure Tsusansho*); and (iii) JETRO, had in effect become the 'Number Two Ministry of Foreign Affairs' (*daini Gaimusho*).

The accusations that JETRO was no longer functioning as a trade promotion organization but was being maneuvred into other areas supports the *Asahi Shimbun*'s contentions that MITI was 'disguising' JETRO in order to continue operations. Also, by alleging that JETRO had become a secondary Ministry of Foreign Affairs *Sankei Shimbun* implied that MITI was using JETRO to wrest away territory form the MOFA.[3,4]

In July 1995, the monthly political magazine *Sentaku* repeated the Triplet story but carried a photograph of *Inside/Outside Japan* instead of JETRO's office.[5] The article, written anonymously, claimed that the reason Triplet was annoyed with Noguchi's article was because JETRO's activities in the United States were a source of irritation to the CIA and FBI. *Sentaku* claimed that the CIA and the FBI were watching closely the activities of the directors of industrial research in JETRO New York when they visited other JETRO offices in the United States. The agencies regarded the MITI officers as CIA-type agents from Japan. The representatives could not be classified as either foreign diplomats or scholars, making their status ambiguous. Also, there was suspicion among members in Congress that the officers engaged in industrial espionage. The article included the information that Masahisa Naito was the first MITI official to serve at JETRO New York as a director of industrial research.[6]

Another article reporting JETRO's involvement in industrial espionage in the United States followed in the 10 October 1995 edition of *Nilkkei Report* followed. Steven L. Harmon reported that the *New York Times* had alleged that the CIA and the National Security Agency had tapped the conversations of Japanese trade representatives and automobile manufacturers during the 1995 trade negotiations in Geneva, providing evidence that Japan was engaging in industrial espionage in the United States. Harmon discovered that the FBI was focusing its investigation on JETRO's offices in Los Angeles and San Francisco, questioning former local staff about their bosses' activities. Harmon revealed that a female staff member had told the FBI that espionage was 'a routine part of the jobs of such Japanese posted in the United States'.

Nevertheless, the allegations of industrial espionage are ultimately of little concern to the Japanese. However, what troubles them is that METI is using public funds to portray JETRO as an import promoter in order to justify its budget, and that METI is using its corporation to expand its territory.

## The skill at disguise (*henshin no gijutsu*)

Chalmers Johnson credited Osaka mayor Bunzo Akuma, the chairman of the Osaka Chamber of Commerce, Michisuke Sugi, and a former official of the Ministry of Commerce and Industry with JETRO's inception in 1951. Their objective was to encourage small businesses to export goods to lucrative foreign markets such as the United States. The organization offered services for export promotion and the provision of information on foreign markets. According to JETRO's website, the organization's first name was the Japan Export Trade Research Organization. In 1954 it was reorganized and renamed the Japan External Trade Recovery Organization.[7]

Johnson wrote that MITI accepted the organization and posted officials in upper management. In 1956, MITI took over and chartered the organization as a Special Corporation, the Japan External Trade Organization. In 1958, JETRO created the Institute of Asian Economic Affairs, which two years later was converted into a public corporation and renamed the Institute of Developing Economies (IDE). The IDE was merged with JETRO in 1998. In 1971 yet another organization was established – the International Economic and Trade Information Centre.

JETRO opened its first overseas offices in the late 1950s, registering it as a public corporation and not an agency of a foreign government under the Foreign Agents Act of 1938, which caused some consternation among American officials. In 1976, the US Department of Justice sued the Japan Trade Council (established in Washington, DC, in 1958) for civil fraud, charging that MITI contributed 90 per cent of the Council's funds through its JETRO New York office. Soon afterwards, JETRO re-registered as a foreign agent.[8]

By 1975, JETRO was operating twenty-four trade centres and fifty-four offices in fifty-five countries, testimony to the fact that not only had Japan become a major player in world markets, but also that MITI was putting down roots overseas. Besides the JETRO offices,

MITI officers were loaned to Japanese consulates, embassies and Japan Chamber of Commerce offices (a chartered corporation established by MITI) located around the world.

MITI made use of the JETRO offices as listening posts, keeping track of foreign trade regulations, foreign and domestic policies that would affect the import of Japanese goods, industrial and environmental standards, government patent applications (in anticipation that new inventions could be applicable to Japanese industries), and investment opportunities for Japanese business. JETRO staff also collected macroeconomic data and surveyed foreign markets on behalf of Japanese small businesses.

By the early 1980s, Japan, whose economy was export-driven, was showing a marked trade surplus with its leading partners, namely the United States, and there was significant pressure from the USA to deregulate domestic markets and raise import quotas for such goods as agriculture, electronics and motor vehicles. Realistically, JETRO's role as a promoter of Japanese exports was no longer as relevant to Japanese businesses as it had been in the 1960s and 1970s. Also, JETRO's role as a surveyor of foreign markets and a collector of economic and political data had, in part, become extraneous, because such research was being conducted by large Japanese multinationals and research institutes and by MITI officers posted in embassies and Chamber of Commerce offices.

However, MITI intended to continue operating a corporation that had effectively resulted in creating more territory for its officials. As a gesture of compliance with US demands, MITI began the process of re-orchestrating JETRO's functions so that the organization would serve as a promoter of foreign imports and foreign investment. According to the 2002 JETRO website: 'JETRO made a 180-degree reversal and began promoting imports entering Japan, a primary mission that continues to this day.'

In 1983, JETRO set up a task force to look at import promotion. In 1984, import promotion activities such as trade fairs were held in Nagoya, Yokohama and Kitakyushu. In the same year, a second task force was set up to promote international economic co-operation for industry. In 1989, MITI completed the conversion of JETRO export promoter to JETRO import promoter, with the establishment of yet another organization, the Institute for International Trade and Investment. The number of foreign offices increased to eighty (has since decreased to seventy-nine) in fifty-seven countries while the domestic offices increased to thirty-eight. At the time of writing, the number of permanent employees is 1,175.[9] JETRO has eight subsidiaries, all of them public corporations. There are nine positions in JETRO that serve as *amakudari* posts, among them two officers from METI, one official from the Agency for Natural Resources, one officer from MOF, and one officer from MOFA.[10]

JETRO claims on its website that its activities focus on supporting imports and investment into Japan 'thereby helping to strengthen harmonious economic relationships between Japan and other nations'.[11] Although JETRO offers free to the public government-generated data on Japan's economy, trade statistics and information on Japanese culture and lifestyles, JETRO's primary image is that of a Japanese government-sponsored organization providing support to business owners who want to export goods and services to Japan.

JETRO's services are directed to small and medium-sized businesses whose owners would like to do business in Japan but who are unfamiliar with regulations, the markets and the consumer culture. From the late 1980s, JETRO began publishing a series of market reports for products that found Japanese consumer acceptance such as foods, alcoholic beverages, clothing, sports equipment, cosmetics, electronic equipment, jewellery and organic produce. More than a hundred reports had been published by the end of the 1990s. Other publications with such titles as *A Survey on Successful Cases of Foreign Affiliated Companies In Japan* and *The Challenge of the Japanese Market* told of businesses that had entered the Japanese market successfully. There are trade directories of Japanese companies who are interested in ventures with foreign businesses. JETRO also offered free consultation services at it offices to prospective exporters. At this time of writing, the market reports can be accessed through the JETRO website.

JETRO offers a number of other support services in Japan to foreign small-business owners. There are trade fairs that focus on specific industries, where businesses can display products and meet potential buyers. There are also the JETRO support centres located in nine Foreign Access Zones (FAZ)[12] providing information to foreign business about Japanese markets, and doing business within FAZ. In 1993, business support centres (BSC) were opened in Tokyo, Yokohama, Kobe, Nagoya and Fukuoka to assist foreign small-business owners during their visits to Japan to find buyers for their products. The BSC offer exhibition space, temporary office facilities and consulting free of charge.

The Foreign Investment in Japan Corporation (FIND) was established as a private corporation in 1993, promoting itself as 'Your Foothold in the Japanese Market'. Its services included the contribution of funds to foreign businesses that wanted to operate in Japan. The corporation claimed: '¥500 million of capital provided by the Japanese government (Structural Fund) and a further ¥445 million was invested by powerful businesses in the private sector and industry association.' Among its thirty-one stockholders were METI industrial associations such as the Electronics Industries of Japan (EIAJ). A METI subsidiary, the Industrial Structure Improvement Fund, was also a stockholder. The majority of private corporations who were investors were in industries that METI regulated. The companies included Toyota Motors, Mitsubishi Chemical Corp., Nissho Iwai Corp., Kobe Steel Ltd and Nissan Motors Corp.

Since the United States is Japan's leading trading partner, JETRO has played an important role for METI. There are eight offices within the United States, while there is only one in the United Kingdom. In 1991, the Senior Trade Adviser Programme was inaugurated in the United States, whereby former executives from Japanese multi-national companies or JETRO staff are posted to the International Economic Divisions of state governments. They visit small businesses operating in their states to find products that would suit the Japanese market. By 1994, there were twenty-one advisers, and by 2000 the number had increased to twenty-seven, providing METI with an extensive network of information-gatherers.

Two new programmes were introduced in 2000. The Tiger Gate Programme introduces Japanese venture capital companies to American incubator-size businesses involved in high-tech areas. JETRO helps Japanese nationals to finance the venture while the tiny companies contribute the intellectual property. The Trade Tie-up Promotion Programme (TTPP) promotes joint ventures between foreign and Japanese businesses via the Internet. Through the JETRO website businesses can find prospective buyers for their products.

JETRO's programmes for the promotion of international economic co-operation range from Japanese language courses in universities to seminars in countries where Japanese university professors and government representatives explain the Japanese economy to foreign audiences. The Japan Economic Foundation (JEC) established by MITI in 1981 is a JETRO subsidiary. *The Journal of Japanese Trade and Industry*, published by the JEC, provides information about the Japanese socio-economic environment and is distributed to organizations and individuals whose interests centre on Japan. The foundation also sponsors joint seminars with foreign governments such as the annual UK–Japan High Technology Forum which is also supported by the British Department of Trade and Industry. Toru Toyoshima, chairman of JETRO in 1993[13] is now the chairman of the JEC. Tomio Tsutomi, a former administrative vice-minister serves as a special adviser.

Although not officially related to JETRO, there are offices of a METI organization called the Manufactured Imports Promotion Organization (MIPRO) in industrialized countries. The organization claims that it was founded 'for the purpose of supporting advanced countries expand their exports of manufactured goods to Japan, thereby contributing to the promotion of international trade and industry'.[14] METI officers who are posted in the JETRO New York office commute regularly to the MIPRO office in Washington, DC.

JETRO's import promotion programmes and literature are packaged to give the corporation a glossy professional image of a Japanese government-supported agency that is earnest in its efforts to help small businesses enter Japanese markets. However, during the 1990s this image became tarnished. Complaints from dissatisfied business owners reporting disappointing results from JETRO's services, and stories by the media of industrial espionage have given JETRO a dubious reputation as a trade promotion organization.

### Does JETRO promise more than it can deliver?

The 16 June 1997 issue of *U.S. News and World Report* continued to probe JETRO's authenticity as an import promoter. An article by William J. Holstein entitled 'With Friends Like These' questioned JETRO's function in the United States. In his article, Holstein described JETRO as: 'a uniquely flexible organization that defies American definition'. He contended that JETRO America did not serve to promote imports into Japan, but rather was a sophisticated commercial intelligence-gathering agency. He suggested that the promotional materials served to disguise the true reason for JETRO's presence. Dr Edward Lincoln, a former advisor to Walter Mondale (former ambassador to Japan), told Holstein: 'At best the Japanese are being disingenuous when they say that JETRO's primary job is promoting American exports.'[15] Lincoln stated that JETRO's 'core mission' was to collect American technology and political intelligence.

When Holstein asked the JETRO New York president Kazunori Iizuka about JETRO's activities in the United States Iizuka insisted: 'We are promoting U.S. exports to Japan to reduce the trade gap between us.'[16] The products representative of small business exports can be seen on the TTPP website. It advertises requests from Japanese companies for such items as 'used medical beds' and 'primary coat stripper for optical cable'.

In his article Holstein stated that there was the risk that products invented by small businesses would be appropriated by Japanese companies to whom they had been introduced to by JETRO. He provided as an example the experiences of a Clearwater, Florida entrepreneur, Donald Lewis, whose electronic device JETRO claimed in its publication *Success In the Making*, that it had marketed successfully in Japan. Holstein contended that JETRO's support led to Lewis losing control over his invention to an automobile manufacturer. Lewis claimed that Toyota had agreed to use his device, and when Toyota had used it for a few days, the Japanese distributor told the inventor that it would be best to sell his stake to Toyota. Lewis felt under the pressure to sell because Toyota was a giant manufacturer and very influential.[17]

JETRO chairman Toru Toyoshima painted a different picture when he addressed an audience of the New York Japan Society in 1993. He reported that a senior trade advisor had come upon Lewis' electronic anti-rust system and thought that it would do well in Japan. According to Toyoshima, the Export–Import Bank of Japan (EXIM) (a METI special corporation that was consolidated in 1998 with the Bank for Overseas Economic Cooperation, also a METI special corporation) loaned Lewis US $1.5 million to expand his operations. Toyoshima said: 'As some of you know, in April 1990 the EXIM Bank of Japan introduced a lending program designed to increase imports into Japan and provide financing to American companies with products that are likely to sell well in Japan. The Florida company became the first to have such financing.'[18]

Karel van Wolferen wrote an article entitled *The Japan Problem* in 1986, when Japan and the United States were engaged in heated trade talks. His article analysed how Japan was dealing with US demands to reduce the surplus by opening up markets to American goods, and stated:

> In Japan quite often – and always more frequently than the West – what is true on paper is not true in practice. Japanese spokesmen widely advertise the fact that a number of foreign firms that have tried hard enough have been successful in this market. These firms are well known because they belong to a small sample always in this context. A select few foreign firms receive assistance to serve as fresh examples of Japanese openness.[19]

The material JETRO has published since 1989 gives a positive depiction of easy penetration of Japanese markets for owners of small business. If they are willing to adapt their products to meet Japanese consumer preferences, and understand the Japanese way of doing business they will experience success like the companies described in JETRO publications.

In 1989, JETRO released *A Survey on Successful Cases of Foreign-Affiliated Companies in Japan*. Claiming that foreign direct investment had been liberalized because the Foreign Trade Control Law had been amended in 1980, JETRO presents thirteen case studies of successful ventures in Japan. The thirteen manufacturers who were questioned about how they had prepared for operating in Japan answered very positively about their experiences. However, they were not identified by company names but by product, location of headquarters, location of operations in Japan, and amount of capital investment.

In 1990 a colourful magazine was issued describing companies that had entered Japan successfully. *The Challenge of the Japanese Market* pointed to companies, such as Baccarat, Bausch & Lomb, Cartier, Jaeger, Peugeot, Rolex and Reebok, that had been accepted in Japan. JETRO did not advise small-business owners that the main reason these companies had successful ventures in Japan was that they already had brand-name recognition among Japanese consumers before entering, and that the Japanese people have traditionally been eager buyers of luxury goods when they travel overseas. The majority of the companies mentioned had originally worked with a large

Japanese trading company which routinely scouted for companies with products that have a ready market in Japan.

The 1996 edition of *Success is Yours* reassures small-business exporters of processed foods that entry into Japan is not difficult if certain procedures are followed. The American confectioner and maker of the famous Jelly Belly jellybeans, Herman Goetlitz, Inc. was held up as an example of how a processed food producer was able to enter the Japanese market successfully. Since Jelly Belly was already popular among Japanese consumers who purchased the product in the United States, Goetlitz could count on instant recognition and success. Also, Sony Plaza (Sony Corporation) was the distributor and would not have taken a risk with a manufacturer that did not have a solid track record. Here again, JETRO did not explain that if foreign businesses do not have a strong brand loyalty among Japanese people before entering the market they will have difficulty surviving unless a Japanese company is willing to take on an unknown. Although JETRO did not participate in facilitating Goetlitz's entry, readers may have assumed that JETRO was involved, since it did not state otherwise.

The JETRO website carries, at the time of writing, 'Success 1996 Case Studies', which continue to tout the success of large foreign companies in Japan that had prior recognition among Japanese consumers before entering the Japanese market. Case study 5 is entitled: 'L.L. Bean Japan Entering the Japanese Market without Capital Investment'. The company's outerwear is popular among the Japanese who have paid extended visits to the United States.

According to the case study, in 1992, L.L. Bean joined the giant retailer Seiyu and Matsushita Electric Industrial to form L.L. Bean Japan. Seiyu put up 70 per cent of the investment and Matsushita the other 30 per cent, the total capital investment being ¥490 million. The study explains that L.L. Bean, a company with a large mail order business in the USA, researched the Japanese market through a consulting firm and found that Japanese consumers preferred retail outlets to mail order. Therefore it had to rely on large companies to market and distribute its goods in Japan. Matsushita imports L.L. Bean goods and Seiyu retails them. Although L.L. Bean did not provide any capital nor did it take any risks, it sold the rights to sell its products to Seiyu and Matsushita, who ultimately control the business in Japan. This type of tie-up is common in Japan, but mainly among well-established foreign companies. Small businesses rarely get the opportunity to participate in these kinds of ventures.

The Foreign Investment in Japan Corporation (FIND) was closed down on 31 March 2002. Edward Lincoln wrote in his book *Troubled Times* that it had been expected that FIND would assist in a concrete way with foreign investment, but the corporation was criticized because it did little more than propose joint ventures with the Japanese firms that were members of FIND. It also charged a fee for the introductions. Lincoln argued that FIND was a government corporation and was therefore not free to give advice on mergers and acquisitions. He concluded: 'Foreign firms were less in need of advice or introduction to potential businesses than in the dismantling of the real obstacles to acquisitions.'[20]

The business support centres have also received poor reviews because they are not centrally located and visitors are few. Foreign business owners exhibiting their goods expressed frustration because few Japanese business owners or potential buyers visited the centres.

The devaluation of the yen and the declining trade deficit with Japan's trading partners may alleviate some of JETRO's burden to continue promoting imports. There is talk that METI plans to phase out some of the import promotion literature and the potential importer data bank, and transform JETRO once again into a promoter of Japanese small businesses. This service would be an effective use of JETRO, but small businesses are ailing and earnest promotion would entail providing substantial subsidies to them to support their efforts – suggesting the use of public funds.

### JETRO's 'core mission': sowing the seeds of a ministry

The thirty-eight JETRO domestic offices and seventy-nine JETRO overseas offices in fifty-eight countries provide METI with an opportunity to post officials in the prefectures and plant a network of METI representatives abroad. The domestic offices, the JETRO support centers and the business support centers act to extend METI's presence throughout Japan. The seventy-nine offices overseas expand METI's territory in Japan because the officials on loan to these offices can perform duties that are also carried out by officials from the Ministry of Foreign Affairs. METI officers, many of whom have received degrees from foreign universities, relate skilfully to foreign businesspeople and government leaders, promoting government economic policy at business and economic conferences and symposiums. Even though they are commercial attachés, METI officials' interfacing duties can give them the semblance of foreign attachés. Most countries post commercial attachés in embassies and consulates. However, Japanese embassies and consulates refer questions regarding business and trade to JETRO. Also, JETRO offices disperse to the public both commercial and cultural information, duplicating some of the literature released by the MOFA.

According to Holstein, JETRO's annual budget for the operation of JETRO's seven offices in the United States was US $30 million.[21] This amount covers the salaries and benefits for local staff but not the relocation expenses of JETRO officers, METI officers or the salaries and relocations expenses of representatives from other government agencies on loan (*shukko*) to JETRO. The sum covers promotional expenses and seminars but not all of the import promotion materials. Nobuya Noguchi told the *Japan Economic Survey* when he was interviewed in October 1995, that 75 per cent of JETRO's budget was taken from public funds.[22] Logically, if METI consolidated some of JETRO functions with the MOFA and MOF overseas operations, some of the offices could be eliminated. For example, the research of foreign political economies by officers in other overseas offices run by ministries such as MOF and by officials in consulates and embassies is regularly contracted to both local and Japanese research and consulting companies, and their reports are transmitted to the ministries' headquarters. Since METI staff are posted in embassies and consulates to cut costs and the drain on public funds they could engage jointly with MOF and MOFA officers in these research projects as well as sharing the duties of interfacing with foreign business and political communities. The Japanese Chamber of Commerce and Industry is managed by METI's Industrial Policy Bureau and, like JETRO, maintains offices around the world. The transfer of some of JETRO's activities to these offices would also serve to cut costs.

Nevertheless, even though opponents of special corporations regard JETRO's duties as extraneous and the offices as 'empty boxes' it is likely that METI will not consider the above options and continue to operate JETRO as its signature piece and one of its power bases in Japan.

# 8
# Conclusion: Non-Performing Reforms

Since the end of the Second World War, Japan has achieved remarkable economic growth. Yet its socio-political system has not developed at the same pace to support the internal social changes that have resulted from this growth. Although their circumstances have changed dramatically, Japanese citizens are still locked into a system that resembles the pre-war model. The ministries concentrated their energies on planning policies that would accelerate Japan's economy to enable the country to catch up with the United States and become a world economic power. Sadly, at that time little analysis was given to how economic growth would affect Japan's socio-political system. An example that aptly illustrates this oversight is the government's allocation of fiscal stimulus packages for public works. Hundred of miles of roads, highways and bridges were built, providing construction companies with lucrative contracts and employment for thousands of workers, but at that time no consideration was given to how the new infrastructure would serve the Japanese populace, let alone the ultimate costs of maintenance. In other words, infrastructure was built for the sake of being built.

At the time of writing the forecast for Japan's future as a global economic power is bleak. The annual economic growth rate during the 1990s was 1.3 per cent compared with 3.9 per cent during the late 1980s. During the 1990s government released ¥120 trillion yen in fiscal stimulus packages, and the Bank of Japan lowered its official discount rate from 6.75 per cent to zero per cent. But none of these measures has so far alleviated Japan's recessive economy.

In 2001, Japan's GDP contracted to 0.5 per cent, the first annual drop in three years. Manufacturing output plummeted to 1.5 per cent from its mid-2000 peak – a thirteen-year low. Property prices fell by 5.9 per cent, the fastest decline in nine years, commercial property falling by 8.3 per cent – 63 per cent below the peak value registered in 1990.

In 2002, Japan's continued deflation took its toll on the real estate market. According to a report released by the Real Estate Economic Institute in January 2003, the number of condominiums sold in Tokyo fell by 0.08 per cent against the year before, marking the third-largest amount since the institute began collecting statistics in 1973. Corporate bankruptcies continued at an alarming rate. It is reported that there were 19,458 corporate bankruptcies caused by the depression in 2002, the second highest in history, and 0.1 per cent higher than in 2001.

News in the financial sector is grim. Mizuho Financial Group, the world's largest bank, reported in January 2003 that its losses were nine times more than had been estimated in November 2002. The bank now admits to ¥1.9 trillion in losses and will attempt to raise ¥1 trillion from outside sources.

The 2002 Assessment and Recommendations for Japan's economy and economic recovery by the Organization of Economic Co-operation (OECD), released in October 2002 projects that Japan's economy will grow by only 0.5 to 1 per cent per annum until the end of 2004, and that because of the general slow-down of the global economy, Japan's deflation will worsen.

In 2002, the government hoped that deflation, the weakening yen and the fact that Japan's trade surplus was steadily decreasing would encourage manufacturers to export more, a strategy that had been fundamental to the planning of economic and industrial policy during post-war economic growth. However, Yasutaru Yamamoto, an economist at the Sumitomo Life Research Institute, warned in his article in the 8 March 2002 issue of the *Japan Times* that dependence on external demand to revitalize the economy would be only a temporary solution. The real problems were structural and unless these were dealt with full economic recovery would not take place.

The OECD report confirmed Yamamoto's predictions. It stated that, in 2002, the appreciation of the yen and the restrained expansion of exports held back economic growth. The OECD recommends that Japan needs to take radical steps to bring about the end of deflation. Moreover, the report stated that the economy could be revitalized if structural reforms were implemented but it also admitted that reforming the system would be difficult because of political opposition and vested interests. The OECD warned Japan that 'there is no more time to be wasted'.

Prime Minister Koizumi has proposed reforms that encompass three areas: (i) fiscal reforms; (ii) state-sector reforms; and (iii) tackling the non-performing loans (NPL). In an effort to reduce public debt, which was 130 per cent of GDP in 2001, 140 per cent in 2002 and in danger of rising to 150 per cent in 2003, Koizumi plans to privatize state-run banks, such as the Postal Savings Agency, and downsize drastically the Fiscal Investment Loan Programme, the two bodies that fund public corporations and public works projects. State-sector reforms also include the elimination of many public corporations. Koizumi is tackling special corporations and chartered corporations first, with plans to privatize them, converting them into independent administrative institutions or dissolving them altogether to ease the flow of public spending. The prime minister's reforms also include the regulation of *amakudari* in both private industry and public corporations.

To date, Koizumi's plans have met with stiff opposition because of the vested interests of the bureaucracy, business and the LDP. Indeed, most reforms have been stymied because of fears that public funds that have continued to flow freely despite the recession will become a trickle. Political bickering among members of the LDP and among members of opposition parties has resulted in political gridlock. In fact, the philosophies of opposition parties that were once at opposite ends of the philosophical spectrum are now converging as the LDP platform encompasses their platforms. The Japanese are in a political limbo.

The staunch support of the LDP by small-business owners helps to sustain the conservatism that permeates the Diet. It was explained in Chapter 5 that small and medium-sized businesses engage in 99 per cent of business activity in Japan, and employ 78 per cent of the work force. Manufacturing businesses, both independently owned and from *keiretsu* groups that rely on procurement contracts from large businesses, are closing because orders have decreased rapidly during the 1990s. To cut production costs the larger firms are procuring cheaper parts from Korean, Taiwanese and Malaysian manufacturers, as well as pulling operations out of Japan and setting up plants in Asian countries where labour costs are far less than in Japan. The hollowing out of Japan spells the disintegration of the *keiretsu* system and painful times for small, independent enterprises that rely on domestic demand.   City

In the mid-1980s, metropolitan and state-run banks pursued small business owners and entrepreneurs with offers of low-interest, long-term loans. Now that banks are calling in those loans and assessing new applications according to stringent regulations, business owners are anxious about how the reform of the Postal Account Agency and the downsizing of FILP will affect their firms. The reform of both institutions indicates to them that loans from such special corporations as the Japan Finance Corporation, as well as other subsidies from the ministries, will be more difficult to secure.

Traditionally, Japanese small-business owners identify themselves with their companies. If they foresee bankruptcy they prefer closing down their operations rather than tying up with other small businesses. Even merging with larger businesses is not normally regarded as an option. Many big business leaders and members of the Japan Federation of Economic Organizations (*keidanren*) support Koizumi's reforms, at least in theory. However, members of the Chamber of Commerce and Industry, whose members are the owners of small and medium-sized businesses have an entirely different perspective on the matter and prefer to support the status quo rather than to risk their families' immediate futures.

### Forecast for Japan: too little, too late?

Until recently, the majority of Japanese citizens were fairly isolated from the political process. They perceived their elite bureaucrats and politicians as being separate from themselves. In general, most voters are reluctant to commit themselves, and they tend to vote for personalities rather than issues. In the early 1990s, there was a concerted movement by politicians during the Hosokawa and Murayama Administrations towards political reforms that could have stopped the evolutionary process of Japan's economic deterioration, but many Japanese people felt that the momentum for change was lost when the LDP returned again to dominate the Diet in 1996. They were discouraged further when they discovered that the public works projects that were receiving funds allocated from fiscal stimulus packages during those administrations had gone over-budget, compelling the government to pump more tax revenue money into the projects.

There are several trends that may point to an increasing awareness of the political process and a growing participation in that process by the electorate: (i) the National Diet sessions are televised daily and voters can observe their politicians; (ii) voters are supporting governors of some of the prefectures such as Nagano and Mie, who are trying to make policies that reflect the needs of their constituents even though the decisions may conflict with the guidance from central government; and (iii) grass roots opposition to unnecessary infrastructure work – but these episodes are still the exception to the rule. Even though there are indications that the Japanese are taking matters into their own hands, no tangible mechanisms exist in the Japanese socio-political system that promotes this kind of participation. The network of interconnecting formal and informal personal relationships between bureaucrats, businessmen and politicians continues, and this organic interdependence paralyses the implementation of policy during a crisis. None the less, these elements are inherent to Japanese society.

Special corporations are illustrative of the basic nature of Japan's political economy. The ministries' determination to maintain territory and thus protect vested interests can be seen in the continued operations of special corporations despite Koizumi's plans to dissolve them. The recession and burgeoning public debt have brought about public recognition that the ministries are using their special corporations for *yokosuberi* and *amakudari* and as monitoring stations in the prefectures, where elite officials from central ministries can influence local government policies. Yet the Japanese defer the administration of reforms of special corporations to their elite bureaucrats.

After Masahisa Naito left MITI on 31 March 1994 he joined Georgetown University in Washington, DC where he took the Marks & Murase professorship as a participant in the Asia Law and Policy Studies program. On 7 April of that year he gave a speech at the Law Center. He reflected on the motivations of ministry officials who worked during Japan's rapid economic growth period and who seemed inspired by their roles as the administrators of Japan's economic

rebirth. He lamented about the change in attitudes of today's bureaucrats, who, he felt, had become inward and 'turf conscious', working
to protect their ministries' territory rather than making policy to
deregulate markets.

Naito told the audience that the Japanese people, who had relied
for centuries on either an emperor or a military regime to govern
them, did not want to take the initiative to plan their own destiny but
preferred to entrust the responsibility to a bureaucracy. He explained
that the submission to bureaucratic rule gave the ministries much
power, which was further enhanced by the close contact between
bureaucrats and businessmen, who feared retribution if they did not
comply with guidance.

The ever-present concern by Japanese, if they do not adhere to
guidance, clearly shows why Japan's existing socio-political system
defies change. The elements explicit to this system are:

(i) a rigid hierarchical socio-political system with a bureaucracy
invested with the powers to plan and implement Japan's post-
war economic growth without being subject to legal sanctions.

(ii) the close co-operation between business, the bureaucracy and
the National Diet that began during the Meiji Restoration. The
finely tuned relationship continued before and after the Second
World War. Known as the 'iron triangle' it is one of the dominant
features of the governing system, in place at the time of writing.

(iii) a conservative political party that has supported the bureaucracy's policies consistently during Japan's post-war period.

(iv) the network of former bureaucrats and bureaucrats throughout
business and government that is perpetuated by the *amakudari*
system, which greatly enhances bureaucratic power to enforce
policy at both the national and local government levels.

(v) significant social pressure to accept bureaucratic policies and
guidance.

Japan's economic woes were originally attributed to macroeconomic
difficulties resulting from inflated real estate and stock prices. The
possibility that structural problems and flaws in the Japanese system
itself were contributory factors was generally not considered until
fiscal stimulus packages not only failed to ignite the economy but
also sent government debt skyrocketing. Japan's prolonged economic

stagnation has finally revealed the fundamental reasons for the inability of the Japanese to take decisive measures to bring about an economic recovery. What we must understand is that in order for substantial reform to occur, Japan's socio-political system must be able to adapt to change – and the process will take many years.

The continuous observation of the conversion process of special corporations can be useful for gauging the progress of structural reforms regarding the civil service system and ministerial power. The streamlining of these organizations may indicate that the bureaucracy is weakening as elected officials push for an end of public funding to public corporations. Similarly, as public debt continues to escalate, the funding available to public corporations will dry up and the organizations will have to find new sources of revenue. However, the most realistic view is that even if some of the corporations are converted into independently administered institutions (IAI) over the long term, they will still receive public funding for years before they become entirely independent of government support.

# Notes

## 1 Introduction

1 An excellent source is *Japan's Policy Trap* by A. Mikuni and R. Taggart Murphy (Brookings Institution Press, 2002), pp. 145–70.

2 In 1989, Karel van Wolferen wrote *The Enigma of Power* (Vintage Books, 1990) in which he expressed his concern about Japan's inability to redirect its export-driven economy towards an economy that welcomed direct investment and more imports, thus alleviating friction with trading partners. 'The phoenix has soared majestically for the entire world to see, and has drawn deserved applause and expressions of awe. But it is burdened with an inherent defect that disorientates it. The defect, of course, is its steering mechanism: in its inability to adapt alternative methods and aims because of the absence of an individual or unified group with the power to make political decisions to shift goals' (p. 407).

3 C. Johnson, *JAPAN Who Governs?* (W. W. Norton, 1995), p. 134.

4 van Wolferen, (1990), p. 11.

5 B. Fulford, 'Japan's half-a-dozen or so big morning newspapers and their affiliated TV networks have deep knowledge of systematic links between government officials, corporations and criminal organizations but they refuse to let the public know, according to more than a dozen senior Japanese reporters and editors' (www.forbes.com/global, 2 February 2002).

6 Bill Whittaker (New York, September 1994)

7 Mikuni and Murphy (2002), p. 41.

## 2 Special Corporations: On and On They Go

1 The Postal Account Agency is a state-run bank. The collection agency is the Ministry of Public Management, Home Affairs, Posts and Telecommunications. The dispersing agency is the Ministry of Finance. Many Japanese prefer to put their money into Postal Savings because the agency offers slightly higher interest rates than do private banks. They also feel more secure because government manages the institution.

2 Yasushi Iwamoto of the Institute of Economic Research at Kyoto University defines FILP. 'The term of Fiscal Investment Loan Program first appeared in the 1953 budget. Since the center of FILP was the first Trust Bureau, we include it in the Trust Bureau system. FILP is a big financial conglomerate operated in the public sector. The largest part is postal savings. Another part is the public pension fund.'

3 *Asahi Shimbun* (28 March 2002).

4 *www.soumu.go.jp/gyoukan/kanri.*

5  *Nikkei Business* (12 February 1997).
6  *Gyoseikan no hoyu suru joho no kokai ni kan suru horitsu.*
7  *Nikkei Business* (12 February 1997), p. 28.
8  K. Tsutsumi, *The Monster Ministries and Amakudari: White Paper On Corruption (Kyodai Shocho Amakudari Fuhai Hakusho)* (Kodansha, 2000), p. 190.
9  Ibid., p. 196.
10  *www.soumu.go.jp/gyousei/kanri.*
11  See Table 2.1 (p. 33) for a list of existing special corporations with number of board members, number of employees, date of establishment, website addresses and annual salaries of the top executive. Please note: the Japan Nuclear Cycle Development Institute (no. 24 and no. 52) is managed jointly by the Ministry of Education, Culture, Sports, Science and Technology and the Ministry of Economy, Trade and Industry. The Japan Regional Development Corporation (no. 43 and no. 61) is managed jointly by the Ministry of Economy, Trade and Industry and the Ministry of Land, Infrastructure and Transport.
12  In December 2002 the restructured DBJ committed ¥10 billion in cash to a debt-equity fund set up to bail out Daiei, the almost bankrupt retail chain. The fund is called the 'Daiei Restructuring Fund', and United Financial of Japan (formed by a merger in January 2002 of Tokai and Sanwa Banks), Mizuho and Mitsui-Sumitomo, three private banks, have committed ¥50 billion for a debt-equity swap, thus mopping up Daiei's debts. United Financial Japan is infusing ¥25 billion and both Mizuho and Mitsui-Sumitomo are infusing ¥12.5 billion each.
13  J. Norwell, 'Bark vs. Bite' *The Oriental Economist* vol. 69, no. 12 (Toyo Keizai, Inc. December 2001), p. 7.
14  Ibid.
15  G. Tett, 'State-funded projects lose £30bn in Japan', *Financial Times* (London: 29 March 2000)
16  K. Iishi, *The Parasites That Are Gobbling Up Japan Dismantle All Special Corporations and Public Corporations!* ((*Nihon wo Kuitsuku Kiseichu Tokushu Hojin Koeki Hojin wo Zenhai Seiyo!*) (Michi Shuppansha, 2001), p. 38.
17  Tsutsumi, (2000), p. 198.
18  See Table 2.2 (p. 43) for a balance sheet showing the profit–loss account for special corporations, where available.
19  T. Kuji, *The Bureaucrat's Kingdom: Japan's Downfall (Kanryo Kokka Nippon no Botsuraku)* (Hihyosha, 1998), p. 104.
20  *Amakudari* is discussed in Chapter 6.
21  The JNOC and *amakudari* is discussed in Chapter 6.
22  Iishi (2001).
23  Ibid., p. 80.
24  Ibid., p. 5.
25  Iishi stated that 40 per cent of the population, or 62,540,000 people, do not work (for example, children, housewives, the aged, the unemployed and the physically and mentally disabled).
26  Iishi (2001), p. 81.
27  Ibid., p. 33.

28   Ibid., p. 26.
29   Ibid., p. 26.
30   Ibid., p. 26 (The position can become permanent, as discussed in Chapter 6.)
31   Ibid., p. 90.
32   The ministries' headquarters are located in Kasumigaseki, a district in Tokyo.
33   *Mainichi Shimbunsha*, 1994.
34   Ibid., p. 183.
35   *www6.xdsl.ne.jp/nomura*
36   See no. 57 in Table 2.1 (list of special corporations).
37   See Chapter 5, note 26, for an example of dam construction.
38   The National Land Agency merged with the Ministry of Construction, the Ministry of Transportation and the Hokkaido Development Agency in 2001 to form the Ministry of Land, Infrastructure and Transport.
39   See nos. 38, 40, 49, and 51 in Table 2.1.
40   www.soumu.go.jp/gyoukan.kanri.
41   www.gyokaku.go.jp/minister/kaiken.
42   www.jetro.go.jp.
43   See Chapter 4, 'The Bureaucracy'.
44   www.kantei.go.jp/foreign/constitution.
45   Information provided by Dr Sadahiko Kano, Professor at the Global Information and Telecommunication Institute (GITI) at Waseda University.
46   These officials, in turn, choose the officials who will work with them (for example, former colleagues).
47   *Mainichi Interactive* (Mainichi Shimbun (4 October 2001).


## 3   The Bureaucracy: Origins of Power

1   I. Murakawa, *Japan's Bureaucrats* (*Nihon no Kanryo*) (Maruzen Library, 1994), p. iv.
2   These elements are discussed in Chapter 5.
3   K. van Wolferen, *The Enigma of Japanese Power* (Vintage Books, 1990), p. 43.
4   K. van Wolferen, 'The Japan Problem', *Foreign Affairs*, vol. 65, no. 2 (Winter 1986/87), p. 290.
5   'Administrative Guidance' (*gyoseishido*) is discussed in Chapter 5.
6   Johnson (1995).
7   K. Calder, 'Domestic Constraints and Japan's Foreign Economic Policy of the 1990s', *International Journal*, vol. XLVI (Autumn 1991), p. 612.
8   www.kantei.go.jp/foreign/constitution/02.
9   A. Mikuni and R. T. Murphy, *Japan's Policy Trap* (Brookings Institution Press, 2002), pp. 40–1.
10   Ibid., p. 38.
11   Ibid., p. 40.
12   J. A. A. Stockwin, *Governing Japan* (Blackwell Publishers, 1975), p. 13.
13   R. Story, *A Story of Modern Japan* (Penguin, 1965), p. 164.

14 The university's name was changed to Tokyo University (popularly known as Todai) after the Second World War. The majority of post-war elite bureaucrats hold law degrees from this university.
15 B. C. Koh, *Japan's Administrative Elites* (University of California Press, 1989), p. 14 Koh wrote: 'The position of the bureaucracy *vis-à-vis* political parties and the Imperial Diet was bolstered by the constitution and practices alike.'
16 M. Muramatsu, *Political Dynamics in Contemporary Japan* (Oxford University Press, 1993), p. 54.
17 J. Sagers, 'The Origins of Japan's Economic Philosophy', *JPRI Critique* vol. 7 no. 9 (Japan Policy Research Institute, October 2000).
18 The English translation for *zaibatsu* is 'financial clique.'
19 Story (1965), p. 103.
20 T. Tsukamoto, 'A History of Japanese Industry' *Journal of Japanese Trade and Industry* no. 6 (1996), p. 44.
21 Tsukamoto (1996), p. 45.
22 Tsukamoto no. 7, (1997), p. 49.
23 C. V. Prestowitz, Jr., *Trading Places* (Basic Books, 1988), p. 229.
24 'Administrative Guidance' is discussed in Chapter 5.
25 T. Nakamura, *The Postwar Japanese Economy* (University of Tokyo Press, 1977), p. 18.

## 4 The Power of the Bureaucracy: The Continuing Saga

1 J. Dower, *Embracing Defeat: Japan in the Wake of World War II* (Penguin, 1999), p. 38.
2 J. A. A. Stockwin, *Governing Japan* (Blackwell, 1975), p. 105.
3 D. Okimoto, 'Political Exclusivity: The Domestic Structure of Trade' in D. Okimoto (ed.), *The Political Economy of Japan*, vol. 2 (Stanford University Press, 1988), p. 310.
4 This is a form of *amakudari*, which is discussed in Chapter 6.
5 *Inside/Outside Japan* (JETRO, New York, September 1992).
6 K. Calder, 'Elites in an Equalizing Role: Ex-bureaucrats as Coordinators and Intermediaries in the Japanese Government Relationship' *Comparative Politics* vol. 21, pt. 4 (1989).
7 The businesses cannot hold investment from a *keiretsu* group.
8 www.jfs.go.jp.
9 Government recognizes the textile industry as a depressed or 'sunset' industry.
10 Dower (1999), p. 532.
11 Johnson (1995), p. 120.
12 S. Yonekura, 'The Functions of Industrial Associations' in T. Okazaki and M. Okuno-Fujiwara (eds) *The Japanese Economic System and Its Historical Origins* (Oxford University Press, 1999), p. 194.
13 Ibid., p. 193.
14 Dower (1999), p. 27.

15  A protectionist industrial policy consists of measures that are employed by a government to nurture the industries deemed important in the national economy. These measures are known as policy instrument or policy tools. In general, the package of instruments includes the regulation of production, the protection of industry from foreign competition through the use of tariffs, tax incentives to companies that procure from domestic manufacturers, subsidies for research and development, and loans for expansion of operations.

16  T. Pugel, 'Japan's Industrial Policy: Instruments, Trends and Effects' *Journal of Comparative Economics* (1984), p. 422.

17  K. Yamamura and G. Eads, 'The Future of Industrial Policy' in K. Yamamura and Y. Yasuba (eds), *The Political Economy of Japan*, vol. 1 (Stanford University Press, 1987), pp. 426–68.

18  Matsumoto was appointed Counsellor in the Embassy of Japan in Canberra, Australia after his book was published, and in 1990 he was appointed as general director of the general administration department of the Japan National Oil Corporation (JNOC).

19  K. Yamamura, 'The Japanese Political Economy after the "Bubble"; Plus ça Change?', *Journal of Japanese Studies* (1997), pp. 301–2.

20  Mikuni and Murphy (2002), pp. 177–81.

21  Ibid, pp. 200–1.

22  Tanahashi is referred to in Chapter 6 in the section '*Amakudari* and *shukko* to Research Institutes'.

23  Mainichi Shimbun editorial staff, *The Kasumigaseki Syndrome* (*Kasumigaseki Shindoromu*) (Mainichi Shimbunsha, 1994), p. 46.

24  Kumano is referred to in Chapter 6 in the section '*Amakudari* to Research Institutes'.

25  Japanese businesses and government agencies are among the clients of the law firm Marks & Murase. It is interesting to note that Carl J. Green, who was the director of ALPS at the time of Naito's professorship, was appointed the senior representative of the Hitachi Corporation in Washington, DC in February 1997.

26  A section of the speech Naito gave at the Law Center on 7 April 1994 is discussed in the Conclusion.

27  Even though Naito was reinstated, albeit not as vice-minister, he still had to contend with rumours of misconduct. According to the March 1996 issue of the monthly political magazine, *Sentaku*, a document was surreptitiously circulated around MITI headquarters, questioning how Naito had financed a restaurant that his wife was operating in the resort town of Karuizawa (p. 47).

28  The ministries call MITI 'notorious MITI' because of the ministry's propensity to pursue the territory of the other ministries. Chalmers Johnson gives a good example of this behaviour in 'MITI, MPT, and the Telecom Wars How Japan Makes Policy for High Technology', found in C. Johnson, L. Tyson and J. Zysman (eds), *Politics and Productivity: The Real Story Why Japan Works* (Ballinger, 1989), pp. 177–239.

29  Nikkei Shimbun editorial staff, *The Bureaucracy: A Creaking Giant Power* (*Kanryo Kishimu Kyodai Kenroku*), pp. 245–6.
30  Mainichi Shimbun editorial staff (1994), pp. 296–308.
31  www.soumu.go.jp.
32  Prime Minister Koizumi was the Minister of Posts and Telecommunications in the former Prime Minister Hashimoto's Cabinet.
33  www.mext.go.jp
34  www.mhlw.go.jp.
35  www.mlit.go.jp.
36  *Asahi Shimbun* 28 March 2002.
37  www.mof.go.jp.
38  www.maf.go.jp.
39  www.moj.go.jp.
40  www.mofa.go.jp.
41  www.meti.go.jp.
42  www.jda.go.jp.
43  www.env.go.jp.
44  I. Murakawa, *Japan's Bureaucrats* (*Nihon no Kanryo*) (Maruzen Library, 1994), p. iii.
45  E. Lincoln, 'Arthritic Japan: The Slow Pace of Economic Reform', *JPRI Working Paper* no. 81 (Japan Policy Research Institute, October 2001).
46  K. Yamamura (1997), p. 325.

## 5  The Interpersonal Networks between Government and Business

1  C. Usui and R. Colligan, 'Government Elites and *Amakudari* in Japan, 1963–1992', *Asian Survey*, vol. XXXV, no. 7 (July 1995), p. 682.
2  K. van Wolferen, *The Enigma of Japanese Power* (Vintage Books, 1990), p.110.
3  R. Osaki, 'How Industrial Policy Works' in C. Johnson (ed.), *The Industrial Policy Debate* (Institute of Contemporary Studies, 1984), p. 49.
4  R. Katz, *JAPAN the System That Soured* (M. E. Sharpe, 1998), p. 170.
5  K. Yamamura, 'Success that Soured: Administrative Guidance and Cartels in Japan', in K. Yamamura (ed.), *Policy and Trade Issues of the Japanese Economy* (University of Washington Press, 1982), p. 99.
6  It is conceivable that the fear of losing administrative jurisdiction over substantial territory may have prompted the continuation of policy.
7  Another example of a cartel club is the Saitama Saturday Club comprising sixty-six contractors based in Saitama prefecture. In May 1991, the Foreign Trade Commission investigated members over suspected rigging. The club has since disbanded.
8  U. Schaede, 'The Old Boys Network and Government–Business Relationship in Japan', *Journal of Japanese Studies*, vol. 21, no. 2 (1995), p. 310.
9  M. Tilton 'Japanese Cartels Still Block Imports', *JPRI Critique* vol. 1. no. 2, Japan Policy Research Institute (October 1994).

10   Katz, R., (1998), p. 45.
11   C. Nakane, 'The Japanese Hierarchy' in D. Okimoto and T. Rohlen (eds), *Inside the Japanese System* (Stanford University Press, 1988), p. 8.
12   The other factors listed were: (i) the sweeping exclusion of the political left from companies and (ii) remarkable differentials of wages and labour between large, small–medium, and small enterprises.
13   M. Matsuba, *The Contemporary Japanese Economy* (Springer, 2001), p. 93.
14   This trend is slowly changing as corporations that are experiencing financial problems bring in fresh talent from outside the organization with the expectation that new strategies will provide solutions.
15   van Wolferen (1990), p. 440.
16   In 1998 there were only sixteen prefectures out of forty-eight that issued local government bonds. These prefectures had enough industry to generate sufficient tax revenue, allowing the coverage of payments when the bonds matured. Local government bonds covered about 8 per cent of public debt.
17   An official from the Kyoto Prefecture Government complained to the author that Tokyo regarded local governments as 'beggars.' According to Chalmers Johnson in his book *JAPAN Who Governs?*, the term '30 % autonomy' also indicates that Tokyo controls local government through the network of officials from the national ministries in local government offices and public corporation branch offices located in the prefectures: 'Another case for concern is the tendency for public corporations to pre-empt the functions of local government in many areas. More and more aspects of daily life have been drawn back under the control of central government, which has given rise to the cynical remark *sanwari jichi* – local government is only 30 per cent independent of national government.' p. 134.
18   www.yomiuri.co.jp.
19   Ibid.
20   van Wolferen (1990), p. 119.
21   Kita-kyushu claims that the first FAZ opened there.
22   www.jetro.org.jp/e/faz.
23   Foreign Access Zone Co., Ltd (October 2000), p. 4.
24   A map of FAZ installations located throughout Japan as well as the addresses can be accessed on www.jetro.org.jp/e/faz.
25   Local government contributes between 20 to 30 per cent to public works projects.
26   By 1999, many prefectures were experiencing the effects of the prolonged recession caused by the sharp decline in corporate tax revenue. In October 1999, the large and densely industrialized prefectures of Osaka and Kanagawa announced that they were on the verge of bankruptcy. Local government opposition to the further construction of infrastructure deemed unnecessary began in rural Tokushima prefecture (adjacent to Ehime) when citizens' groups protested about the construction of a dam because they were concerned that the prefecture, already ¥60 billion in debt, could not afford to carry the 20 per cent share of the cost

with central government. Construction often goes over budget thus increasing the costs. The governor, a member of the LDP, was in favour of the dam, but 95 per cent of Tokushima residents voted against the dam in a referendum. Nevertheless, the Ministry of Construction vowed not to accept defeat and to carry on with the project. At this time of writing, construction has not commenced.

27  The executive directors of the larger of the JETRO overseas offices are METI officials who are usually aged forty or a little older, and are considered to be elite. While Iga's son was at JETRO he became friends with the executive director. Coincidently, the executive director became the director of the Import Division in MITI's International Trade Administration Bureau, which participates in the administration of FAZ.

28  The seat at JETRO New York was moved to JETRO Hong Kong in 1999 after Iga lost the gubernatorial election.

29  K. Calder, 'Elites in an Equalizing Role: Ex-bureaucrats as Coordinators and Intermediaries to the Japanese Government–Business Relationship', *Comparative Politics*, vol. 21, pt 4 (1989).

30  Tsukuba University is a national university focusing on the sciences and receiving substantial funding from government for research.

31  K. Oyama, *A Political Economic Study of Administrative Guidance (Gyoseishido no Seiji Keizai Gaku)* (Yuhikaku, 1996), p. 38.

32  Professor Masafumi Matsuba, Professor of Economics at Ritsumeikan University, defined small businesses in his book *The Contemporary Japanese Economy* as having a capital investment of less than ¥30 million. (Springer, 2002), p. 178.

33  Japantimes.co.jp (15 November 2001).

34  Ibid.

35  MITI managed foreign exchange until 1964.

36  E. Lincoln, 'Arthritic Japan: The Slow Pace of Reform', *JPRI Working Paper* no. 81 (Japan Policy Research Institute October 2001).

## 6  The Ties that Bind: *amakudari* and *shukko*

1  www.jinji.go.jp/jinzai.

2  It must be emphasized that there is a vast difference between the lives of the rank-and- file bureaucrats, who work without compensation, and the elite officials, who receive far higher salaries and ample rewards after retirement.

3  www.asahi.com (December 2002).

4  C. Johnson, *MITI and the Japanese Miracle* (Stanford University Press, 1982), p. 68.

5  T. Kuji, *The Bureaucrat's Kingdom: Japan's Downfall (Kanryo Kokka Nippon no Botsuraku)* (Hihyosha, 1998), p. 94.

6  Ibid., p. 89.

7  The bank co-operates closely with METI for the small business sector.

8  Kuji (1998), p. 82.

9 Ibid., p. 118.
10 See Chapter 2 for information regarding the JNOC.
11 Komatsu had retired from MITI in 1986, moving to the recently privatized Long Term Credit Bank of Japan as an adviser. He then became a member of the board of directors at Nissho Iwai, later climbing to the position of vice-president, and on to that of chairman.
12 See Chapter 4: 'Japanese opinions of their bureaucracy'.
13 K. Tsutsumi, *The Monster Ministries and Amakudari: White Paper on Corruption* (*Kyodai Shocho Amakudari Fuhai Hakusho*) (Kodansha, 2000), p. 197.
14 Ibid., pp. 147–8.
15 Ibid., p. 324.
16 Mainichi Shimbun editorial staff, *The Kasumigaseki Syndrome* (*Kasumigaseki Shindorumu*) (Mainichi Shimbunsha, 1994), pp. 202–3.
17 Tsutsumi (2000), p. 145.
18 See Chapter 4, 'Japanese opinions of their bureaucracy.'
19 D. Okimoto, 'Political Inclusivity: The Domestic Structure of Trade' in D. Okimoto (ed.), *The Political Economy of Japan*, vol. 2 (Stanford University Press, 1988), p. 316.
20 Mainichi Shimbun editorial staff (1994), p. 262.
21 I. Murakawa, *Japan's Bureaucrats* (*Nihon no Kanryo*) (Maruzen Library, 1994), p. 79.
22 F. Jains, *Local Government and Policy Making in Japan* (New Delhi: Commonwealth Press, 1987), p. 16.
23 Ibid., p. 14.
24 Council of Local Authorities for International Relations (CLAIR), *Local Government in Japan* (Tokyo: CLAIR, 1999), p. 7.
25 Mainichi Shimbun editorial staff (1994), p. 258.
26 Ibid., pp. 273–5.
27 Murakawa (1994), p. 78.
28 Tsutsumi (2000), p. 138.
29 See Chapter 4 for references to Matsumoto in 'The bureaucracy.'

## 7 The Japan External Trade Organization: The Scent of a Ministry

1 See Chapter 2, 'Independent administrative institutions: more image than substance?'
2 See Table 2.1 on page 33.
3 Ironically, Noguchi, a MITI official, had been loaned to JETRO from 1986–9, when he served as the Director of the Planning Division. He returned to MITI for two years before being loaned to JETRO San Francisco where he served as president for three years. He moved directly from San Francisco to New York to take the president's post for two years.
4 The day after the article appeared Komori was called to the offices of JETRO New York at 6 pm after most of the staff had departed. Noguchi or his superiors in Kasumigaseki may have expressed displeasure to the *Sankei*

*Shimbun* because they saw the article as a personal attack on Noguchi. The paper did not print further articles on the subject.

5   *Sentaku* (Tokyo: July 1995), p. 86.
6   See Chapter 4: 'Japanese opinions of the bureaucracy.'
7   www.jetro.go.org.
8   C. Johnson, *MITI and the Japanese Miracle* (Stanford University Press, 1982), pp. 231–2.
9   See no. 50 in Table 2.1 (p. 33).
10  www.6.xdsl.ne.jp.
11  www.jetro.org.jp.
12  www.jetro.org.jp/e/faz
13  See Chapter 2 for details of Toyoshima '*Amakudari* to special corporations and public corporations.'
14  MITI Handbook.
15  W. J Holstein, 'With Friends Like These', *U.S. News and World Report* (16 June 1997), p. 48.
16  Ibid.
17  Ibid., pp. 47–8.
18  *Inside/Outside Japan* (JETRO New York, November 1993).
19  K. van Wolferen, 'The Japan Problem', *Foreign Affairs*, vol. 65, no. 2 (1986/7), p. 293.
20  E. Lincoln, *Troubled Times* (Brookings Institution, 1999), p. 192.
21  Holstein (1997), p. 46.
22  'Nobuya Noguchi on How Small U.S. Companies Get Help from JETRO on Cracking the Japanese Market'.

# Bibliography

Bailey, P., *Postwar Japan 1945 to the Present* (New York: Blackwell, 1995).

Calder, K., 'Elites in an Equalizing Role: Ex-bureaucrats as Coordinators and Intermediaries in the Japanese Government Relationship', *Comparative Politics* vol. 21, pt 4 (New York: 1989 July), pp. 379–403.

Calder, K., 'Domestic Constraints and Japan's Foreign Economic Policy of the 1990s', *International Journal* vol. XLVI (Autumn, 1991).

Dower, J., *Embracing Defeat: Japan in the Wake of World War II* (New York: Penguin, 1999).

Iishi, K., *Bureaucrat Heaven: The Bankrupting of Japan* (*Kanryo Tenkoku Nihon Hassan* (Tokyo, Michi Shuppansha, 1999).

Iishi, K., *The Parasites That Are Gobbling Up Japan: Dismantle All Special Corporations and Public Corporations!* (*Nihon wo Kuitsuku Kiseichu: Tokushu Hojin Koeki Hojin wo Zenhai Seiyo!*) (Tokyo: Michi Shuppansha, 2001).

Jains, F., *Local Government and Policy Making in Japan* (New Delhi: Commonwealth Press, 1987).

Japan External Trade Organization, *A Survey on Successful Cases of Foreign-Affiliated Companies in Japan* (Tokyo: JETRO 1989).

Japan External Trade Organization, *The Challenge of the Japanese Market* (Tokyo: JETRO 1990).

Japan External Trade Organization, *Success is Yours* (Tokyo: JETRO 1996).

Johnson, C., *Japan's Public Policy Companies* (Washingtan, DC: AEI Press, 1978).

Johnson, C., *MITI and the Japanese Miracle* (Stanford: Stanford University Press, 1982).

Johnson, C., 'MITI, MPT, and the Telecom Wars How Japan Makes Policy for High Technology', in C. Johnson, L. Tyson, J. Zysman (eds), (Ballinger, 1989).

Johnson, C., *JAPAN Who Governs?* (New York: W. W. Norton, 1995).

Johnson, C., 'Japanese "Capitalism" Revisited' *JPRI Occasional Paper No. 22* Japan Policy Research Institute (Cardiff, CA: 2001 August).

Katz, R., *JAPAN the System That Soured* (New York: M. E. Sharpe, 1998).

Koh, B. C., *Japan's Administrative Elites* (Berkeley: University of California Press, 1989).

Kuji, T., *The Bureaucrat's Kingdom: Japan's Downfall* (*Kanryo Kokka Nippon no Botsuraku*) (Tokyo: Hihyosha, 1998).

Lincoln, E., *Troubled Times* (Washington, DC: Brookings Institution Press, 1999).

Lincoln, E., 'Arthritic Japan: The Slow Pace of Economic Reform' *JPRI Working Paper No. 81*, Japan Policy Research Institute (Cardiff, CA: 2001 October).

*Mainichi Shimbun* editorial staff, *The Kasumigaseki Syndrome* (*Kasumigaseki Shindoromu*) (Tokyo: Mainichi Shimbunsha, 1994).

Matsuba, M., *The Contemporary Japanese Economy* (UK: Springer, 2001).

McNamara, R., *In Retrospect: The Tragedy and Lessons of Vietnam* (New York: Random House, Inc. 1995).

Mikuni, A. and Murphy, R. T., *Japan's Policy Trap* (Washington, DC: Brookings Institution Press, 2002).

Murakawa, I., *Japan's Bureaucrats (Nihon no Kanryo)* (Tokyo: Maruzen Library, 1994).

Muramatsu, M., *Political Dynamics in Contemporary Japan* (Oxford: Oxford University Press, 1993).

Nakane, C., 'The Japanese Hierarchy' in D. Okimoto and T. Rohlen (eds) *Inside the Japanese System* (Stanford: Stanford University Press, 1988), pp. 8–14 (reprinted from Nakane, C., *Japanese Society* (Berkeley: University of California Press, 1970)

Nakamura, T., *The Postwar Japanese Economy* (Tokyo: University of Tokyo Press, 1977).

*Nikkei Shimbun* editorial staff, *The Bureaucracy: A Creaking Giant Power (Kanryo Kishimu Kyodai Kenryoku)* (Tokyo: Nikkei Shimbunsha, 1995).

Norwell, J., 'Bark vs. bite' *The Oriental Economist Report* vol. 69, no. 17 (New York: Toyo Keizai, Inc. December 2001).

Okimoto, D., 'Political Inclusivity: The Domestic Structure of Trade' in D. Okimoto (ed.) *The Political Economy of Japan*, vol. 2 (Stanford: Stanford University Press, 1988), pp. 307–53.

Osaki, R., 'How Industrial Policy Works' in C. Johnson (ed.) *The Industrial Policy Debate* (San Francisco: Institute of Contemporary Studies, 1984), pp. 47–70.

Oyama, K., *The Political Economics of Administrative Guidance (Gyoseishido no Seiji Keizai Gaku)* (Tokyo: Yuhikaku, 1996).

Prestowitz, C. V., *Trading Places* (New York: Basic Books, 1988).

Pugel, T., 'Japan's Industrial Policy: Instruments, Trends, and Effects' *Journal of Comparative Economics* (1984) pp. 420–35.

Sagers, J., 'The Origins of Japan's Economic Philosophy' *JPRI Critique* vol. 7, no. 9 Japan Policy Research Institute (Cardiff, CA: October, 2000).

Schaede, U., 'The Old Boys Network and Government–Business Relationship in Japan' *Journal of Japanese Studies*, vol. 21, no. 2 (Seattle: 1995), pp. 293–317.

Stockwin, J. A. A., *Governing Japan* (London: Blackwell Publishers, 1975).

Story, R., *A Story of Modern Japan* (London: Penguin Books, 1965).

Tilton, M., 'Japanese Cartels Still Block Imports', *JPRI Critique* vol. 1 no. 2, Japan Policy Research Institute (Cardiff, October 1994).

Tsukamoto, T., 'A History of Japanese Industry', *Journal of Japanese Trade and Industry* nos. 6 and 7 (Tokyo: 1996, 1997).

Tsutsumi, K., *The Monster Ministries and Amakudari: White Paper on Corruption [Kyodai Shocho Amakudari Fuhai Hakusho]* (Tokyo: Kodansha, 2000).

Usui, C. and Colligan, R., 'Government Elites and *Amakudari* in Japan 1963–1992', *Asian Survey*, vol. XXXXV no. 7 (Berkeley: July 1995), pp. 682–98.

van Wolferen, K., 'The Japan Problem', *Foreign Affairs* vol. 65, no. 2 (New York: Winter 1986/87).

van Wolferen, K., *The Enigma of Japanese Power* (New York: Vintage Books, 1990).

Yamamura, K., 'Success that Soured: Administrative Guidance and Cartels in Japan' in K. Yamamura (ed.), Policy and Trade Issues of the Japanese Economy (Seattle: University of Washington Press, 1982), pp. 77–109.

Yamamura, K., 'The Japanese Political Economy After the "Bubble"; Plus Ca Change?', *Journal of Japanese Studies* (Seattle: 1997), pp. 291–331

Yamamura, K. and Eads, G., 'The Future of Industrial Policy' in K. Yamamura and Y. Yasuba (eds.), *The Political Economics of Japan*, vol.1 (Stanford: Stanford University Press, 1987), pp. 425–68.

Yonekura, S., 'The Functions of Industrial Associations' in T. Okazaki and M. Okuno-Fujiwara (ed.), *The Japanese Economic System and Its Historical Origins* (Oxford: Oxford University Press, 1999), pp. 568–85.

# Index